THE DISENGAGING INFLUENCES

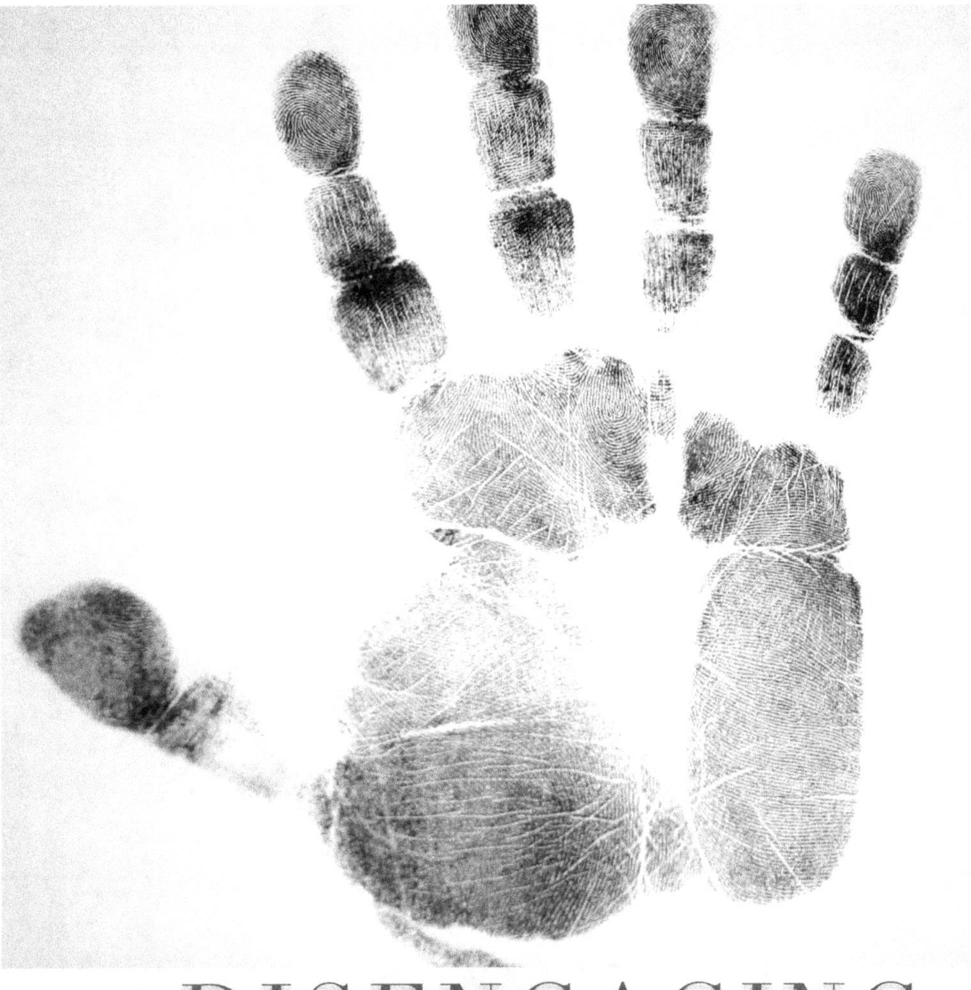

IMPRINT YOUR LEARNING

Make training memorable and effective for businesses

DEDICATION

Dedicated to those that saw the potential in me and encouraged me in my pursuit towards it:

PJ, Pajarito, Kezza and Bluey

CHAPTER 1

NEW ROLE

"Great news Philip, we want you to head up a new division for the company that will drive us forwards into the next era of our growth."

"Sounds interesting," Philip replied. "What will the division do?"

"Well," started Gareth, the long serving Chief Operations Officer for Woodroot Hosting Inc. "The Board need us to focus less on selling hardware and more on selling web services. They believe that this is where the real opportunities lie over the next few years. What we are not sure about, however, is whether we have the right people to effect this change."

"The right people?" responded Philip. "What do you mean?"

"I mean, we are not sure whether the people we have got are capable of making the change in terms of selling and supporting this new direction," stated Gareth with a touch of concern beginning to creep into his voice.

"So, are you looking to ME to be the one to fire people?" Philip exclaimed. The element of concern reflected in his voice now. "I've never managed anyone before, let alone fired them for lack of capability."

Gareth allowed a wry smile to creep over his face.

"No Philip, that's not what we are looking for you to do, well, at least not initially. The Board have always praised your ability to 'wow' customers and influence them, particularly when presenting solutions and going for that sale. In fact, when you spoke at the East coast conference last May, they thought you were outstanding. You captivated the imagination of the audience and were really entertaining."

"So what has this to do with the new division? Do you want me to set up something to entertain the staff?" he joked, but half-wondered if that was where Gareth was going with this conversation.

"Well, something like that," Gareth replied. "We want you to set up a new training function for the company. We have never had one before because we have always made the point of recruiting people that can already do the job, but these are different times, Phil."

"But why ME?" Philip exclaimed. "I've never trained anyone in my life! I wouldn't even know where to start! I'm just a sales guy, not an entertaining guru for training!"

"I appreciate that, Philip, but you're the man for the job, we know you are. Like I say, training is all about keeping people entertained and having some fun and we *know* you can do that really effectively. We want you to start thinking about this immediately."

"But what about my current proposals I am working on, and my existing customer-base? I can't just abandon them," Philip pleaded. Moving out of his comfort zone had become an alien concept to him.

"We've made arrangements for Kirsty to take them over. Over the next week, you'll need to contact your customer base and formally handover to her, please. Phil, in your new role, you'll be reporting to me so feel free to come to me for any guidance on strategy or corporate direction; but I'm going to need you to write a proposal document that I can take to the board showing how you'll go about this new challenge and what resources you reckon you'll need. OK?"

"When do you need that by?" asked Philip.

"I could do with it for the next Board meeting in a fortnight."

"But I have no idea where to start."

"I'm sure you can work it out Philip."

"But what if I can't?" Philip was beginning to get a bad feeling about this now.

"Let's cross that bridge if we should ever come to it, ok? Now, I need to go to a meeting Philip. See you in a fortnight...with your proposal."

And that was how it all started. In that short conversation, Philip's world had been turned upside down. He had been in sales for a decade now and had never entertained any thoughts of ever leaving it. He was old enough to have enjoyed some amazing experiences in sales, winning several sales competitions that had taken him on exotic trips abroad. He had been asked to speak at a conference following a remarkable sale he had enjoyed with a customer that now represented over 25% of the total Woodroot Hosting revenue. With a regular, steady income the net result of that sale, Philip was able to relax in his role of sales executive, his quarterly targets were always well within his reach. He enjoyed the thrill of the chase, though. Getting the customers' signature on the contract was always exhilarating, and he loved the ecstasy when he finally processed an order. Thinking of Gareth's comment about his presentation skills, Philip realised he always got a buzz when he presented the solutions to a board or panel of customers. It was true, he *was* thrilled by his performance at the conference. In fact, after his presentation delegates approached him and eulogised over his wit and humour, always good for the ego. Philip found that enjoyed the limelight, but didn't need it, or crave it. There were others that seemed to monopolise the conversation with stories of their escapades at parties, but Philip was not like that. He preferred to be *invited* to speak about his experiences through fear of appearing boastful. In a period of deep reflection, he once mused that this was the result of his upbringing with a mother that always voiced a hated of arrogance in anyone.

Over the years of his working life, Philip had always risen to a challenge. If his sales manager had set him the task of increasing his sales by a ridiculous figure, he had always put in the extra effort to achieve it. He realised that he did this, not out of a fear of losing his job or any negative motivation. Instead, he knew that he his energy was the result of him relishing the opportunity to break new ground, to do something he had never done before and push himself. He had been a strong athlete whilst at college, always above average, but never settling for second place. He had trained himself, always focussed on achieving perfection, always looking for improvement in himself. But with this, came a self-critical nature. When he played football matches, although he loved to win, the result was less important to him than his personal performance. He would self-analyse after every game, knowing when he had given his all, and when he could have done better. The trouble was, when he walked from the field feeling he had not been on top form, he would spend the night lying in his bed, mentally agonising over his performance, feeling wretched and realising he could have done better. He hated to let himself down, Philip hated to fail. It was his greatest weakness. He would throw himself into a venture with all his energies, but when he felt failure was on the cards (due to his deficiencies) he would get frustrated and angry with himself.

But he never walked away from a challenge. He would always face up to his losses, and enjoy the wins when they came along. Being aware that failure and success teetered on the same knife-edge, prevented Philip from ever being arrogant or over-confident. His father, Jack, whom Philip admired, was a fine, reliable man would always offer a quiet word of advice if Philip ever looked like boasting about his achievements. Jack was equally quick to praise his son too, though, and it was for this reason that Philip had always felt he could come to his father with his life issues.

As Philip sat in his apartment and thought through these matters, he realised that he hadn't needed his father's advice for a long, long time. Several years had passed since they had enjoyed (if that was the right term) a genuine heart-to-heart. After all, Philip was one of the top account managers at Woodroot Hosting since his 'big sale' a couple of years ago. Thinking about those years since he had landed the contract with *Braxted Online*, Philip realised that he had not really been challenged or stretched in his career recently. He had fallen into a 'comfortable' pattern of working life, with regular orders coming in that he didn't have to work too hard to gain. He had enjoyed maintaining the relationships with his customers on the golf course or entertaining them at sporting events and exhibitions, but he had not *developed* himself much in that time. Why would he? Life was good; life was comfortable.

But now; now he was thrust into unchartered waters. Now he was well outside of his comfort zone and his mind had gone completely blank over what to do next. He was out of practice, he thought. He hadn't done anything 'new' for too long and, as a result, he didn't know where to start. Grabbing his laptop, Philip opened it and ran an internet search on *'training'*.

'Perhaps Mr Google might be able to point me in the right direction and help me understand what this 'training' thing is all about?' Philip thought.

1,790,000,000 results came back to smack him in the face and shout at his inexperience. He needed to refine his search, but how? He had no idea what words to use and he suddenly felt completely overwhelmed. For the first time in his career, Philip felt he was looking down the barrel of the gun, facing personal failure. His next move was going to make or break his career.

CHAPTER 2

JACK

Philip didn't sleep much that night. As he tossed and turned in his bed, his mind was racing with fears and concerns over where to start with his new role. Questions fired through his head like: 'Do I need a team?', 'Where am I going to train people?' and 'Do I train people in sales skills first or should I do technical training?' 'Is training about entertaining people?'

Something that Gareth had said during their conversation that day didn't sit well with him, but he wasn't sure what it was. The more he thought about it, the more his mind seemed to get twisted and caught up in the immensity of it all. So many results from his internet search must mean that this was a huge ocean that he had been asked to swim in, and he didn't know the first thing about survival in a sea of training.

Before finally drifting off to sleep, Philip resolved to get help and elected to make the call to set up a visit to his father. He knew that, once upon a time, his father had done something like this before, though he was never entirely certain what his father did for a living!

"Dad, I'm in a spot and I need your advice?" he asked, causing his father's interest to pique.

"What's up son?" asked Jack trying to hide the tone of concern in his voice and remain as cool as a man of his years could be. Jack was not a tall man, but looked fit and healthy, despite his now white hair and a complexion that showed his age.

As Philip recounted the conversation he had had with Gareth, Jack's body language relaxed with relief. As a parent, hearing that your son was in trouble always sent ones mind spiraling to imagine the worst, so Jack was relieved that it wasn't anything life-threatening, at least. He was touched with appreciation that his high-flyer of a son, who seemed to be 'making it' in the city, had turned to him for advice in his time of need.

"I haven't a clue where to start, what to do, or how to go about this challenge, Dad," concluded Philip. "I've never trained anyone before, never even thought about it, if I'm honest."

"Yeah, but you've attended training courses before, right?" enquired Jack.

"Sure I have."

"So, tell me," he asked. "Have you ever walked away from a training course and thought to yourself, 'that was really useful'?"

"Not really, Dad. Most of the training I've been to has been from old men that don't live in the *real* world," Philip replied.

"That's a good start then Phil; tell me why you felt that they didn't live in the 'real world'?"

"Hmmm," he contemplated. "Well, I think it was because the examples they used were not relevant to what I do. I mean, they would talk about computing like it was something new, with dial up connections to the internet and programmers writing in MS DOS!"

"I have no idea what that means, but no matter. What did you feel that you *needed* out of the training that you didn't get from these instructors?"

"I suppose that I wanted to be inspired, to feel motivated to implement new ideas or ways of working, or at least to learn something I didn't know before! Most of what they had to say, I reckoned I could have read in book or watched a video online, so I began to wonder why I needed some bloke to lecture me in the first place!"

"That's an interesting term you use there son, why do you say they 'lectured' you?" Jack seemed to indicate to Philip that this line of questioning was making progress, so Philip played along with the conversation.

"Well, most of the training I have been on has been like I was back at school: the teacher doing the majority of the talking, reading from slides. It was boring and I caught myself on several occasions lamenting the fact that I was imprisoned in this room, rather than out in the field, selling and making money."

"Ahh, now we are getting somewhere. Think about what you've just said to me Phil, you've probably got some really key things there."

"But," started Philip. "The training was rubbish!"

"Exactly!" responded Jack calmly, smiling at his boy. "So you know what you need to avoid. Think about it, son. You've told me that the training was pointless to you because it didn't hit your needs. You didn't learn anything new, so you started to wonder what was the point of it? and maybe you questioned whether you had been told to go on the wrong course? You needed something that the trainers didn't give you. You weren't at all engaged in the learning, and that means it was a waste of *your* time and *their* money."

Philip nodded in agreement. What his father was saying was making complete sense, as usual.

"Your lesson is right there, Phil. Make sure the training you offer is going to be of value to the audience. What is it that they need to learn *and* can take back to use in their job? What is it that you can give them that is going to make a difference to them and help them improve?"

As Phil reflected upon this conversation with his father, he started to feel that there was something in what his father had said. Maybe he could make a real impact on the company by getting the employees to work differently, better or more efficiently. What could he do to improve the capability of the staff at Woodroot Hosting? At the back of his mind, Philip thought about the sales people he had been on customer meetings with. He had always felt that their questioning skills were weak, whereas this was something he considered to be one of his areas of strength.

As he broke out of this reflection, Jack asked: "I can see you're thinking about something there Phil, what's going through your mind?"

"I was thinking that the questioning skills I've seen in the sales guys could be better."

"OK, so what are you going to do next?"

"I just feel as though I am like a blind man stabbing in the dark, hoping to hit my target. I'm out of my depth, Dad. I don't *know* what to do next!" Philip said in a worried tone.

"I understand, son," Jack consoled. "Nobody *knows* how to do a job unless they are trained to do it, though. It's then that you either learn how to do the role, or you realise that what you were doing already was the right thing all along."

"You think I should go on a training course to learn what a trainer does?"

"That's one option, I suppose," stated Jack. "But you could also find someone to act as your mentor. That way you can learn through doing it; on the job learning, as it were."

"Is that what you used to do when you were working?"

Jack chuckled before responding. "After all these years son, you still don't know what I did for a living?!"

"I've never been sure, sorry Dad."

"No worries. I worked at a water purification plant Phil, I wasn't a 'trainer', but I was responsible for ensuring that my team were able to do the job I asked of them and that meant that I sometimes needed to 'train' them. Other times, I knew that they had the knowledge to do the job, but lacked the confidence in their ability to apply that knowledge. In those circumstances, all I had to do was to tease the answers out of them. In that respect, I guess I could call myself a 'mentor', yes."

"What would a mentor do for *me* though?" Philip asked whilst also thinking who he could possibly get to act as his mentor. He didn't know any trainers very well, and those that he had come across in his working life, he didn't consider very effective.

"Well, I suggest that there are two criteria that you need to look for in someone that can help you, Phil. Firstly it is someone that knows their stuff, has been in the field of expertise you are looking to move into and so is sufficiently knowledgable. That way they can act as your sounding board when you come up against problems or generally hit a brick wall in your own knowledge. You can go to them with the scenario you're experiencing and they can help you find the right solution. At least, that's what I found when I first went into management."

"That's a challenge in itself, Dad. I don't move in those circles, I don't know *any-one* that might fit that criteria."

It was as if Philip was thinking out loud as he then asked: "What is the second criteria? You said there were *two*?"

"There are. The second criteria is really very important. If you are going to learn, you need to find the right person to learn from. This is not just about their experience or their theoretical knowledge, but also about the person they are, their character. You see, you'll work best if you find a mentor that you can *trust*, Phil. You need to find someone that you know has *your* best interests at heart and you aren't left contemplating whether they have a hidden agenda or an ulterior motive for helping you. Those are the two things to look out for Phil: *knowledge* and *trust*. You'll know the right person for you when you find them."

"But *where* can I find a mentor for my situation, Dad? I don't know anyone!"

"I can't help you with that, son. That person you'll need to find for yourself. Just keep an open mind, Phil. Mentors can come into your life from situations you would never have expected."

"OK, but in the meantime, I'm just going to have to get on with it, I suppose. Gareth and the board have faith in me, and reckon I am more than capable of doing this job, so maybe I should just do something similar to what I did at the East Coast conference. After all, that's why they offered me the job."

"You do what you need to do son, but don't forget what you told me needs to be avoided, based on your own experience of training. Oh, and keep your eyes and ears open for that mentor. If you are going to make a real go at this role, you'll need one, just like every top tennis player has a coach, you'll need someone to give you some direction."

CHAPTER 3

FIRST BLOOD

From his own experience, Philip knew that the sales people at Woodroot were notoriously poor at fact-finding from their customers. He had been on enough joint sales calls to confirm that the vast majority of them needed work in questioning the customer to identify their deep-rooted needs *before* trying to sell them something.

Sensing that he could get a 'quick win' with Gareth, he elected to run a training session on questioning skills and went to the monthly sales managers meeting to tell them that he expected all of the sales people in the company to attend it.

"Another training session on questioning?" sighed Sasha when Philip told the group of his plan. "Shouldn't we be learning the features and benefits of the new offering instead?"

"Nope," responded Philip curtly. "There's no point learning about the products if you don't ask the right questions to open up the chance to talk about them. So I expect to see *every* sales person at the training this Friday."

"Friday isn't a great day for training, Phil," Guy started to suggest before being shot down by Philip, who was starting to get a little tetchy that he was being questioned like this.

"Look, I have the backing of the board for this and it is important to the company that they attend, so that's the end of it." Philip turned on his heels and strode out of the meeting room, leaving the managers to the remainder of their meeting.

Questioning techniques were Philip's major strength and he knew it. He could train them in his sleep, he knew precisely how to ask all the right questions at the right times and so it made perfect sense to train the sales people on something that was well within his specialist area. He would be good, he knew it. He would be able to make the training relevant to the needs of the Woodroot Hosting sales force and in so doing he would overcome the issue he discussed with his father, Jack. He also had some great jokes to throw at the audience and Philip was confident they would walk out of the room having been thoroughly entertained, whilst having been shown exactly how to improve.

Over the preceding days before the training session, Philip focussed his time and thoughts on his accounts, working with Kirsty to set up appointments with the larger customers for a personal handover. He decided to work on his training session on Friday morning, that would ensure he dealt with the important things first, like his customers, for the majority of the week. After all, his training session was all in his head anyway. Philip was confident he could deliver this training in his sleep.

Friday morning came and Philip was having a good week. He had managed to contact the majority of his accounts to tell them of his move into training. Some he had managed to speak with personally, others he had emailed or left voice messages on their phones with the information that their account manager was now Kirsty. So, now, Philip could spend time thinking about the training session with a clear conscience, his 'proper' work was done.

He was sitting at his desk, hurriedly scribbling down some notes (mainly his jokes) in preparation for the afternoon event, when Sasha strode up to him.

"Have you got a minute?" she asked in an expressionless manner that gave nothing away. Puzzled over why Sasha had sought him out, Philip got up from behind his desk and suggested that they go to get a coffee from the coffee machine at the other side of the office. Once there, Sasha looked concerned as she took her cup from the machine.

"Philip, it's about your training this afternoon," she started. "I know I voiced my concerns to you at the meeting earlier this week, but I just wanted to explain myself in more detail."

"It's alright," declared Philip. "I know what you're going to say, you think that they have had quite enough training on questioning skills to last a lifetime and that you'd rather they spent the afternoon selling."

"Actually, I..."

"Let me just explain something to you, Sasha," Philip spoke in a slow, slightly patronising tone that clearly highlighted his annoyance and frustration at being challenged. "I have been asked by Gareth to gear up the staff ready for this change in direction. He has left decisions on *what* I train and *when* I train, to me. As such, I have decided that, without sufficient skills to open the customer up to our new products, there is no need to learn product features and service costs. I hope you appreciate that I'm simply 'putting the horse well and truly before the cart'!"

"I understand what you are saying Philip, it's just that…"

"I'm glad you understand, Sasha. Now, I really need to get on as I am delivering the session this afternoon and I need to prepare. Thanks for your concern, I appreciate it." With that, Philip turned his back on Sasha and walked back to his desk, without turning back to see the frustrated and annoyed look on her face.

It didn't take long after he settled back at his desk before Philip's phone rang. It was one of his favourite customers with whom he had shared several happy rounds of golf over the years. This customer had been sent an email to explain that their account was being transferred to Kirsty. Higher-valued customers were receiving personal attention from Philip in the form of telephone calls and meetings, but since he wasn't on that list, Philip hadn't spoken with him.

They chatted for the next hour like two old fiends (some of the conversation was related to work, but mostly they spoke about golf); then Philip looked at his watch and realised with a jolt that he was nearly late for the training. Making his excuses to the customer, he dashed to the meeting room and was met with several glaring eyes from a disgruntled salesforce. A quick glance at the numbers indicated that roughly half of the sales people were in the room.

"Where is everyone?" Philip asked the group.

"Half of my team are working from home today; they always work from home on Fridays so that they can get their admin done," replied a tall, mature man with a bushy mustache. Philip didn't recognise him. "I thought Sasha told you?"

"No, she never said a thing about it," Philip snapped back.

He was annoyed that, having spoken with him earlier, she had never said a word about the fact that half her team weren't going to come to the training anyway. Perhaps, he thought, she had told them not to come because she wasn't committed to the topic he was training them on? That must be it, he decided, she had been against it from the start and now she was making a stand through her team. He would be certain to mention what she had done to Gareth afterwards.

Just then, a couple more sales people walked into the room saying: "Sorry Philip, we are on a conference call to a big customer and need to get back to it. We can't make the training today, I'm sure you understand. The customer must come first, right?"

Just as quickly as they appeared, both of them left. Philip felt himself getting angry by the fact that here he was, trying to help these people, and they were not even prepared to turn up. He resolved to put all his efforts into training those that had actually made the effort to be there; he felt that he owed them that much at least.

"Before you get going Phil, what time will be finish?" asked one of the most successful sales people in the company, Kathryn. Philip knew that, of all the sales people in the organisation, Kathryn was one of the least likely to benefit from this training on fundamental questioning skills.

"Yeah, it's Friday man. End of the week Phil. Is there any chance we can get off early?" asked Henrik, another of the high flyers that Woodroot boasted.

From that moment onwards, Philip struggled to maintain control of the room. At times, he felt as though the whole group were working against him or, at least, were trying to antagonise him by asking leading questions to get him off track and have a laugh at his expense. Even *his* jokes failed to land well with the group, failing to produce the raucous laughter that he had envisaged. When he asked the individuals to break into pairs and practice the questioning model he had presented, he was sure he heard someone say: "this is ridiculous, what a waste of time!"

Philip was exhausted as he sat in the room, alone and dejected. The training had not been taken seriously by any of the salespeople that had actually bothered to turn up. Several of the group had left before the session had finished, citing various excuses to leave the room. Philip sensed that the mood in the room was, at best, disinterested in the topic he was training. Several of the attendees even looked as though they may have been snoozing when he was telling them about the questioning model he had used to great effect when he was out in the field, selling.

As he reflected upon his performance, Gareth came striding into the room confidently, shutting the door firmly behind him.

"A word please Philip," he demanded. Then, without waiting for a response, Gareth stated: "I've just spoken with Kathryn, Henrik and a few of the others that you had in here all afternoon. Why have you taken some of my *best* salespeople out of the field, when they could have been making money for the company? I understand you decided to teach *them* the most basic sales skills? You *do* appreciate that these are some of the best sales people that have ever worked for this company, and you are wasting their time in here? They could be teaching *you*, for goodness sake!"

"I thought that everyone would benefit from improving their questioning skills," Philip stammered, sensing his day was about to get even worse.

"Did you seek any advice on that decision, or even talk to anyone about it?"

"Er...yes, well...kind of. I mentioned what I was doing to the sales managers earlier this week."

"Yes, I know you did and I also know that Sasha tried to tell you what a bad idea it was, but that you didn't listen! Philip, do you realise that these managers are your stakeholders for this training and *they* tried to explain to you the folly of your plan? I understand that Sasha even came to you this morning to say that half her team would not be at the training because they were working from home, but you just blew her off before she had a chance to tell you? Philip, you need to listen to these people, *they* are your customers now, they can help you or they can hinder you and right now you've made them all question the value you bring to them and their teams."

"What do you mean, they are my *stakeholders*? and they can *'hinder'* me? I thought I was working under your authority and that the board were behind me?"

"They are Philip. You have to understand though that we *need* to make a very real impact on the market as soon as we announce the changes to our product offering. I need our customers to be getting calls from highly skilled and *motivated* employees of Woodroot Hosting and, I'm sorry to say, that group of people who have just left this room, are certainly *not* motivated employees."

Once more alone, Philip put his head in his hands. Questions were buzzing around his head like annoying flies that couldn't be swatted away. Could things get any worse? Why had he been so arrogant and not listened to Sasha? His mother would be so ashamed to have seen the way he dismissed the sales managers and treated Sasha. Why had his training session fallen so flat? Why had all the participants been so reluctant to learn? What did he need to do now, to pull things around? He wasn't even sure he had answers to *any* of these questions, nor would he ever have. He felt the full weight of the role on his shoulders now. Philip knew he was out of his depth.

That night, he lay in his bed and thought about his week. He recalled the words of his Dad, Jack: *'Find someone to act as your mentor'* he had said. *'They can be your sounding board, they can help you find the right solution'*.

As Philip eventually drifted off to sleep, he resolved to step up his search and do exactly as his father had suggested, but first he needed to talk with Gareth and find out exactly what he wanted to see him achieve in the role.

CHAPTER 4

MENTOR

"What do you mean, *'What do I want them to do differently?'* I want them to sell solutions not products. We've had this conversation before Philip, please don't make me repeat myself."

"I appreciate that," retorted Philip. "But what I need to know is what represents success to you, and the Board? I mean, how do we know whether I've done a good job for you or not?"

"Whilst that's a good question, Phil, I don't have the time to think about such things and, quite frankly, I think that's something we might expect *you* to be telling *us*. Perhaps you'll have a think about it and put it in that proposal you're supposed to be giving me this week? Now, if you'll excuse me, I need to get on."

This was now the second encounter Philip had experienced with Gareth that indicated he was getting tetchy and annoyed with his lack of knowledge or competence. Was that normal? Or was it just highlighting his lack of experience and ignorance? Philip felt as though he had hit yet another barrier and was once more at a loss of what to do next.

"Thanks for arranging this meeting," Kirsty said as Philip drove to his handover meeting with his top client. *Braxted Online* had been Philip's biggest customer for the last few years and had shown tremendous loyalty by renewing their business each year. They were the key to Philip's success as a salesperson at Woodroot Hosting.

Philip was naturally concerned about handing over his most precious customer, but he also knew that the relationship he had built up with Mo and Ashley, the co-founders and owners of the business, was strong enough to withstand a change in personnel, especially as Philip was still working at the company.

"It's always good to see you Phil, but what is it that you wanted to talk with us about today?" asked Ashley.

"I wanted to personally introduce you to Kirsty as I thought I owed it to you to meet face to face. There are some changes happening at Woodroot, Ash, and I have been asked to take on a different role in the company which means that I won't be able to look after your account any longer, unfortunately."

"Oh, that's too bad," responded Mo. "What role are you moving into?"

"I've been asked to set up a new training division for the organisation, but, if I'm honest, and I know I can be with you guys, I am a novice at this and am really not sure where to start."

"Wow, that's a career change right there!" Ashley stated. "I didn't see *that* coming! I remember when I was asked to move away from television technology to computers, it was pretty daunting," he empathised.

"Well, times have to move on, buddy," Mo chipped in. "Tell you what though, why don't I hook you up with our Learning & Development Manager, María, for a chat? She may be able to give you a few pointers and ideas, she is pretty switched on," suggested Mo. "She's been with us a few years now, and I have to say she is a great asset to the company."

"Oh that would be great!" Philip immediately replied, sensing potential relief at the thought of talking to someone actually doing the role he was supposed to be in.

"No problem, let me see if she is available right now, and maybe you can have a chat with her whilst we bring Kirsty up to speed with how we operate at Braxted?"

María was not at all what Philip expected when they were introduced. All the trainers he had met in the past were 'ancient has-beens', men and women that had seen better days, and still lived in them! María, though, was younger. She was probably a similar age to Philip, attractive with long black hair that was tied back in a ponytail. She wore a black pencil skirt and a white blouse that looked thoroughly professional, but remained utterly feminine. Philip didn't know whether her youth and beauty were a good thing in her role, or if it was and indication she might lack experience and credibility. He elected, however, to keep an open mind and see what she had to say. After all, Mo and Ash had personally appointed her and given her a terrific recommendation, and Philip trusted them.

María and Philip chatted for a few minutes over a coffee, talking through the usual social topics in order to get to know one another. He was struck by how comfortable he felt in her company and how easy it was to talk with her about anything. She had a warm smile as she spoke that encouraged Philip to speak candidly and openly to her. She had followed a similar career path to him (initially in sales before being moved into a training role). María stated that she had found developing people to be a better 'fit' to her talents than sales, though.

"Interesting. How is it a better fit for you, María?" Philip asked, eager to ascertain whether he could assess his skills similarly.

"Well, in sales, I was great at building relationships with people, but not so great at closing the deals. My customers loved me because I was empathetic with them and understood when they had genuine reasons not to buy. My bosses were frustrated that I didn't push them for an 'uncomfortable close', but that never felt right to me. At one performance review, my manager asked me where my career was going and I responded that I was happy just to 'drift along' and continue doing what I was doing. He was an astute man and told me that he had enrolled me on a training course, and that I was to go to it with an open mind. He told me to let him know what I thought at the end of the training when I returned to work. As it turned out, it was a 'Train the Trainer" workshop. The course was good, but what sold me was this. The first thing that the trainer said to us when the course opened was: *'You are all sales people, you have the skill and knowledge to sell ideas, concepts and products to individuals. As a trainer you are using exactly the same skills, but you are now selling the idea of change to a group!'* and with that, I was hooked," María explained.

Intrigued and sensing the relevance of this conversation, Philip asked her what she did with this knowledge after the course and what she did next.

"I realised that this was what I wanted to do in my career and I started to do some training sessions for sales people. I soon realised that because I understood the role of sales people, I could relate to their experiences and design sessions that could help them improve their abilities. That helped me figure out how to make sessions relevant and valuable for them to invest their time"

"That's really interesting, María and that's pretty similar to where I find myself," Philip stated, before explaining to her his current challenges and what was concerning him. "I think I have realised that I need to provide training that is relevant to the audience, but I am struggling with how to also make it relevant to the needs of the organisation as well, María. I suppose I am struggling because I don't really know what the organisation expects of me!"

"Ah, I see your predicament Phil," María empathised. "It sounds similar to when I took my first 'full-time' training role in a manufacturing company. I've an idea, Phil, why don't I have a think about things that might help your situation and maybe we can meet up later this week so I can take you through them? Some of my experiences and what I have learnt over the years in Learning & Development might help you?"

"Great idea! Yes, I'd like that," Philip greedily accepted, realising that here, at last, was a person that might be able to guide him in his new role.

CHAPTER 5

FOUNDATIONS

With sandwiches being toasted and coffee cups on the table in front of them, Philip sat opposite María in a pleasant coffee shop, eagerly awaiting the opportunity to learn from her. He noticed how nice she looked, her dark hair cascading over her shoulders and her brown eyes sparkling whenever she looked at him. She had greeted Philip as if she had known him for years, with a typical European kiss on each cheek, and Philip immediately felt a bond of trust growing between them. He sensed that she would do nothing to harm his career.

They chatted about their backgrounds and how radically different, yet similar they were. María, originally from Spain, had come to this country over ten years ago in search of opportunities and work. She had tried hard to lose her Spanish accent, though there were still some traces and tell-tale signs remaining. Philip, on the other hand had a completely different background. He was born and bred in this country and had never moved away from his home town (other than to go to University). They had both taken sales roles directly after graduating their degrees and enjoyed some success in their careers, without believing themselves to be outstanding; and now they were both to be in a training function. The sole difference seemed to be that one had been 'guided' towards this route, and the other had it thrust upon them.

"I'm really keen to hear what you have to say that might help my situation, María," Philip eventually blurted out, somewhat clumsily. Sensing that he might have sounded a little aggressive, he immediately felt awkward. He had cut short her stories of her hometown in Spain to direct the conversation back to work.

After a momentary pause, María flashed him a winning smile and said: "I've had a think about what I have learnt over the last few years in this role and I've got something to show you that I reckon explains what I have experienced quite neatly. It's really all the things that I've discovered to be bad practice in training, the pitfalls if you like. I call them the five *'Disengaging Influences'*," said María as she took out her notepad and pen from her handbag.

María proceeded to draw a triangle on the notepad. "A friend of mine from University went into forensic science and was always talking about how amazed she was that all fingerprints were so similar, yet different. I thought to myself, we all have our own unique fingerprints that leave an invisible trail behind us wherever we go. Training people is pretty similar, we leave a print of ourselves on those that we train, our own 'fingerprint' on their memory. It's up to us to make certain that the learner doesn't wipe that print away before it becomes an indelible part of them. It sounds poetic, but does it make sense?"

Philip nodded in agreement and offered his own understanding to ensure they were in fact on the same page. "It makes for a beautiful simile," he stated. "I think you are saying that just as a fingerprint is left on a glass table, for instance, so we can etch the learning into people's brains so that they think or behave slightly differently?"

"Sí, that's it. Leaving a fingerprint is nothing more than an impression of the friction ridges of a finger, she told me, and in the same way, we need to leave an 'impression' in the minds of the people we train."

"But you said they were *dis*engaging influences? What do you mean by that?"

"They are *disengaging* because any one of these five elements, or 'fingerprints'," she smiled at her analogy as though it had just dawned on her, "will prevent you from being effective in developing employees. We are in a position to touch the lives of the people we train, but whether we do, or not, is dependent upon our skill and ability."

"So, if there are five of them, that's essentially a *hand* print then?" Philip joked.

"I guess so!" María laughed. "We can call this your *'handprint to success'* if you like!" she jested. "Anyway, I then got to thinking about my first training job, Phil, and it was awful. It was because of my experiences in that role, that I started to realise what the connections were and why our training was so poorly received by the employees. In all honesty, I think it was down to my boss, Jim, a truly arrogant man." Maria looked away shaking her head very slightly.

Philip thought back to his most recent conversation with his own manager, Gareth, and wondered whether there may be a similar story from María.

"Please go on," he prompted, leaning in towards her, eager to learn from her experience.

"Jim was always neglecting the most fundamental part of what we do. He spent no time with the business and therefore failed to understanding what the *organisation* needed. He never *asked* people where they thought personal development was required. Instead, he *told* them; and that was the same as the way he dealt with his team." Philip could sense his cheeks reddening with embarrassment at the realisation that this was precisely what he had done over the matter of training the sales people last week.

"I remember going to meetings, watching him *tell* management what was lacking in their people knowledge and skills, based on no data, no research, nothing factual. He would then get us to design training programmes around his self-imagined needs. The end result was that we delivered training that the employees didn't want to attend *and* found completely useless when they went back to work. Us trainers were so embarrassed; can you imagine standing in front of a group of disgruntled delegates, delivering something you had no faith in?"

Philip did just that. He sensed the discomfort, the embarassment and unprofessionalism María and the team must have experienced.

"When the training was evaluated, we all became utterly dejected. Often the feedback was 'yes we know what the theories are, we have been doing this for years. Teach us something we *don't* know!'"

Philip grimaced, reflecting on both last weeks' training and his own experience of attending irrelevant training courses. He recalled one occasion he found so frustrating that he ended up turning on his laptop and spending 5 of the 8 training hours replying to emails in silent protest; on another, he found himself struggling to stay awake, let alone focused.

Maria continued to relay her experience, "I suppose what I learnt from this experience is that, at the very heart of all that we do, should be research and analysis. I mean, we should know *exactly* what we are expecting to change as a result of the training we conduct, and what 'good looks like'. I think Stephen Covey in his book '*The 7 Habits of Highly Effective People*' stated that we need to 'start with the end in mind', yet many times I have been in the situation where, what we expect to see change, is fuzzy and blurred. The greatest problems I have experienced have been caused by a **Lack of Research**." As María spoke, she wrote these words at the base of the pyramid.

"I think we need to research on at least one of the *three* levels, Phil," she continued. "*Organisational, team* and/or the *individual*."

Philip reflected before saying: "What do you mean? To research at all of those levels before doing any training sounds like we will be spending a disproportionate amount of time collecting information from too many places!"

"I'm not saying we need to research *all* of these areas for one piece of training. What I am saying is that we need to identify which of them is our main target for the training."

"I see. Is it easier if we just pick one and focus on that?"

"The thing is, they are all interconnected," she paused. "Or at least they *should* be. If we understand the strategic changes needed for the *organisation*, the timescales within which the change needs to be effected *and* how to measure it, then we have a great frame of reference for our training."

"That's a big 'IF'," declared Philip.

"Sure it is, but if we have those parameters in mind it makes it easier to look at how that change translates into the *team* environment, and then cascades down to an individual level."

"That makes perfect logic María, and sounds easy when you put it that way."

"It can be, if the flow is in that direction. Very frequently, though, we have to work from the *individual* level, upwards, which is possible, just more challenging."

"I can imagine," Philip reflected.

"Only once we have considered the impact of the training at these levels, can we have a good understanding of the '*training need*' we are working to solve. It is the only way for us to be effective as a function. Does that make sense, Phil?" she asked.

"Yes, I think so," replied Philip. "If I understand you correctly, you are saying that if we don't know how the training fits into the corporate strategy for the organisation, for instance, then there is a massive chance it will land badly with the employees."

"Ultimately, yes!" Maria smiled. "But it's not just limited to the *corporate* strategy. All Managers of teams will also have their own strategy for success and you'll need to ensure your training fits into *their* plans too. That way you represent an enabler to their success and one that they will want to work with because you will solve problems for them."

"That makes a lot of sense when I think about the training that I've been forced to attend over the years and how I've got little, or nothing, valuable from it." Philip took a sip from his mug as he considered for a moment.

"I have a question though," he said. "What do you do when Senior Leaders tell you to 'just train people on something, *anything*'? I mean, sometimes the request for training isn't clear, or seems a bit feeble because of a lack clarity. What do you do then?"

"That's a great question," responded María. "And one that I come across quite frequently. Managers will come to me and ask me to 'do some training' because their team haven't had any for a while or they need to ensure they feel as though they are 'progressing'. This is completely the wrong reason for taking people away from their work and it makes *us* look unprofessional for facilitating it too. If we agree to train under these circumstances, Phil, it's likely we are setting ourselves up to fail, so we need to be the expert here and stand firm. I've told managers that effective *learning* generally happens when we can measure the impact of the training."

"Ahhh this is really relevant to me at the moment," exclaimed Philip. "My boss has told *me* to work out how to measure the impact of the training! All that they seem to be interested in is selling a solution, having previously only sold products."

"That's a good place to start then, Phil. You see, if you know the number of sales that the company, or a team have targeted, whether volume or revenue, that's a good foundation to work from. Success of your training can be measured by whether or not that target is achieved. Of course, there will always be a question over whether the training was a direct or a contributory factor to that achievement, but that's for another discussion. The key here is to identify your *stakeholders*, whether they are managers, senior executives or the company as a whole. Then, manage that relationship throughout the process, which starts with understanding what they *need*. It's just like what we did when we were in sales, really."

"OK," said Philip, in a reflective mood, tucking into his food. "Already I have realised where I have gone wrong. It makes a lot of sense to do your homework before committing to any form of training. I understand that now. If we don't know why we are training something, then there isn't much point in doing it, we are shooting in the dark. I've had recent experience of the after-effects of that and it was non too pleasant!" he said. Then he added: "So if we have got that information, what do we do with it?"

"That's a good way of putting it and you've already started to think about the next stage, Phil," declared María. "Once you have the objective, the next question you need to ask yourself is: *'is training the answer?'* In other words, will training solve the problem or is it better to employ a different solution?"

"No, you've lost me there! I don't understand that," said Philip as he stuffed a large mouthful of tuna melt.

"Let me tell you another bad experience I had. I was asked to train a bunch of technical programmers, you know high-tech, geeks, the sort of guys that wear tee shirts and shorts with flip-flops all year round? Well, I was asked to train them on a new code of conduct that the company had to roll out as part of their compliance training. As this only applied to this group it was pretty bespoke, but I didn't look at it that way. Instead, I prepared the classroom training in the same way that I would for anyone else. It was a disaster. I fell flat on my face, Phil, and got some really bad reviews as a result."

"Why? what did you do wrong?" asked Phil, surprised.

"I had assumed that everyone learns in the same way. I had assumed that techies enjoy classroom training in the same way that, say, sales people do, or any other role for that matter. It wasn't until one of them turned around to me at the end of the session and stated: *'I don't see why we couldn't have done this online!'*; then I realised that there are more ways to deliver training than just in the classroom. You see, some people learn better alone, through self-study, whereas others need people around them to bounce ideas off. Some enjoy and learn from reading or e-learning; they enjoy looking at a computer screen, like these high tech geeks. Others respond better to videos or personal interaction. In fact, most of us learn from actually *doing* the job. We learn a lot from our personal experiences." She nibbled a piece of her ham and cheese sandwich before continuing.

"There was some research done by McCall et al. in 1988 and also Robinson & Wick in 1992 that concluded we learn about 10% of what we know from formal learning, whereas approximately 20% comes from interactions with other people (co-workers and our bosses). They found that the vast majority of our development, around 70% actually, is the result of on-the-job experiences."

"Really? That much?" Then Philip thought, "Well, actually, when I think about it, I would agree that I've learnt most of what I know from experience out in the field. I've made mistakes and then learnt not to do things again," he declared.

"Absolutely," agreed María. "Most of what I am saying to you now is the result of *my* personal experience and the mistakes I made whilst actually doing the job."

"Cool, so if that is the case, why do we even have a training department at all? I mean, we could just get employees to learn everything on the job, couldn't we?"

"Well, we could, but there is potential for that to be quite costly and very time intensive. You see, development, whether on the job or in a classroom, can be quite a painful experience because it can involve us making mistakes before learning from them. If those mistakes were made whilst you are actually doing your job, rather than in the safe environment of a training room, the impact could have substantial ramifications on sales, business efficiencies and customer relationships."

"So, are you saying that the role of training could be to play out different scenarios and see how people adapt and react to them?" suggested Philip.

"Yes, partly," stated María. "It's not always possible to play out every scenario, but our job is this; we need to facilitate people making the connections in their brain between good theory and good practice. We can provide the opportunity and occasion to try things out in a safe environment, so that when it comes to reality, they are prepared with the right response, to some extent anyway. This creates efficiency and shows high levels of professionalism. Think about a top footballer. They will go to training every day and be taught, through drills and exercises, to make the right decisions in matches, to know when to attack and when to defend, when to make the darting run into the box and when to hold back. Perhaps there is never a point in time when they can categorically state that their brains are 'programmed' to make the right decisions, but the training is designed to make the process quicker and easier when they are in a game."

Philip was lost in the simile. As an avid footballer, María had just impressed him with her apparent knowledge of the sport and how the 'beautiful game' should be played.

"After the training, people won't necessarily appreciate that their ability to think so clearly, or react so quickly, was the result of their *training*. But it's a proven fact that the training increases their skill levels to the point where we call it 'natural ability'."

"That's fascinating," said Philip as he mentally digested the concept. "At our firm, they once spoke about generating a 'coaching culture'. Where might *coaching* fit into this process?"

"Another great question Phil. Coaching is usually an 'on-the-job' form of development. It would fall into the 70% bracket, according to that research. Sometimes, it's better that an 'independent' person coaches the employee. I say 'independent' in that they are not formally managed by the coach. This sometimes helps the coachee to open up and be honest about things without the fear of being judged or jeopardising their careers. Anyway, we are getting away from the point Phil. Let's deal with coaching further down the track. To summarise this stage, I call this 'disengagement', **Ineffective Design of Training**," said María as she wrote the next tier on the pyramid diagram.

"You've already given me a lot to think about María and I feel as though there is still a lot more for you to share with me."

"Sí, you're right," María replied. "Perhaps you can go away and have a think about what we have discussed in terms of your new role, then let's get together again to look at the next steps and the next *'disengagement'*?"

"Great idea. I will need to pin Gareth down on his expectations first I think, and then give some further thought to the best way to go about training people within Woodroot Hosting. Thanks so much María, you've been a great help to me so far, I really appreciate it."

"I'm happy to help. Call me if there is anything you'd like to run passed me, or if you need some clarification on what we have talked about today?" she offered.

"Definitely," he replied, sensing now that he had a 'safety net' in María that would give him confidence to get things right. As they parted, Philip strode away with an added spring in his step. He felt his world was a better place now that María was in it.

CHAPTER 6

RESEARCH

Over the following few days, Philip collected information. He did little other than ask questions and listen to the responses. As a result, he gathered a firm understanding of the expectations from the Board in terms of two issues: the revenue targets for new sales of solutions over the forthcoming 12-month period and secondly, a latent target that came out of left field. Apparently, there were concerns that staff morale would be greatly impacted as a result of the announced changes. The senior leaders were not willing to entertain the idea that the company would drop out of the running for the corporate engagement award nominations which they had enjoyed over the last 7 years. This was an independent survey conducted across a variety of companies that the staff members completed anonymously, and had become a gauge by the company of employee engagement. Some senior executives had even indicated that they saw the new training function having a direct impact on staff morale and would be looking to this survey as an indicator of Philip's success. Philip was so glad to discover this now, before he started, rather than have it sprung on him at a later date, he thought.

Philip's research also provoked him to discuss the potential changes from the managers perspective in the business. This raised some interesting anomalies. Philip had found that the Sales Managers feared the change from the perspective of their team members struggling with skill issues. They had got used to selling a product through glossy brochures, with structured pricing guides, and now they would be walking into client meetings not having a clue what the customer might need or what products may help them. Their sale was to become more of a process of discovery, rather than a clear product sale. By contrast, when he had spoken with the Support Managers, their concerns were over internal communication with the sales teams. Support were worried that the sales people would sell solutions that they could not realistically support, without heavy investment into new infrastructure or staff. They told Philip that they did not want to be seen as the 'bad guy', causing the sales person to have to go back to the customer with bad news that what they had promised, could not be delivered. Finally, the back office staff were concerned what might be the repercussions from a financial and a people perspective. Emile in Finance stated that the finance teams needed to be clear about costings for the solutions and should be involved as early in the sales process as possible to guide the sales teams to make a profit. Emile also highlighted that discounts needed to be closely monitored to ensure that profits were forecasted correctly and the company not placed into a significant loss on any one deal. Sunette, the HR manager, had very different concerns because she stated that the changes might impact anything from salary expectations of current and future staff, to recruitment issues, as her Talent Acquisition team would be looking to recruit from an unfamiliar market pool. Like the senior executives, she also shared significant concerns over the impact of staff morale on the engagement survey.

With all this information, Philip's head started to spin. How would he ever be able to design a training course that might satisfy *all* these issues and keep everyone happy? Did he need to prioritise the most important team, and ensure that the training fitted *them* at least; and then hope that the others might be able to work out which bit of the content of the training was right for *their* business unit? Which were the most important teams anyway?

As he sat in the staff café, Philip stared at his blank notebook and wondered, once again, where to start. The heavy feeling returned to him once again as Philip felt the weight of this immense undertaking weighing on his shoulders. Perhaps, he thought, this was way beyond his abilities. Did he need a team of trainers? Could he justify numerous salaries knowing that this would put further pressure on the profits of the organisation? But, being a competitive individual with the stubborn streak he got from his mother, Philip was not about to give up. He took out his phone and dialed María's number.

"Hi María, I'm sorry to bother you, but I really need your guidance again."

"No problem Phil, it's good to hear from you again. How's it going?" she asked.

"I've managed to collect a ton of information from all around the business, but none of it seems to tally or agree! Managers of each unit don't share the same concerns and none of their worries seem to line up with the strategic direction of the organisation. I don't know where to start or how to move what I've gathered into the 'design' stage." The tone of Philip's voice was beginning to sound stressed as he explained the issue to her.

"OK, well you've nailed the first stage by the sounds of things, Phil."

"Eh? What do you mean 'I've *nailed* it?'" he asked incredulously.

"It's essential that the business areas feel as though they have been listened to, and understood, before we present the training plan to them. This is going to be just like a sale, Phil. You've spent time understanding the current situation and the problems that they foresee for their specific units. So, when you present your solutions to them, you can present reasons why you are training this or that, because it will be based upon *this* research. Well done!"

Philip would hear from her tone that these words were genuine and he felt reassured that his work was moving in the right direction. He was still in a kind of mental fog though, and didn't quite know where this was, in fact, heading.

"Next steps then Phil," she continued. "I suggest that you get a blank sheet of paper and draw out the process of a sale from start to finish, including the post-sales support, where finance and personnel fit in, on so on. Then, once you've got that nailed, overlay the issues that you've collected from your interviews with the managers and staff."

Philip had started drawing this out in his notebook as María was talking. He begun to see that there was a plan beginning to form. He drafted out the issues for each stage as they chatted through them on the phone.

"OK, so I was thinking that I should design a training course for the most important group in this process," he explained. "Looking at this, it seems that the most important group are sales because that is where it all starts. So, should I design something that is appropriate to *their* needs and hope that it satisfies the needs of the others too?"

"I think you can do better than put out some training and simply 'hope' it works!" María spoke with a reassuring tone. "Think about what our conversation over coffee the other day, Phil. If you train the first group in the process to do their job effectively, but the other groups are not able to support that process because *their* training was inadequate or not relevant to their roles, what would be the outcome?"

"I guess the whole thing would come crashing down like a house of cards!" replied Philip, again feeling the sense of overwhelming hopelessness.

"You're probably right," María replied, a tone of empathy in her soothing voice. "So what you need to look at is not ONE course, but MULTIPLE courses. Remember, everyone learns in different ways. Think in terms of the 70-20-10 principle too, Phil. Not all the training needs to be *delivered* by you, but you can support the managers and individuals' learning on the job."

"Yes, you're right María. I suppose I was thinking of getting as many people in the room at the same time so that I could say that the training has been 'done'."

"It's a good job you called, Phil. I've come across many managers that have told me to 'do training' to their teams. They seem to think it is a box that they need to check before they can get on with their 'proper' work. Sadly, they don't see it as a valuable enough exercise to spend the time on getting it right. For them to start seeing *value* in what you do, you'll need to provide training that is *tailored* to their needs, not a 'one size fits all' approach."

"You're right María. I have to write a proposal for Gareth by the end of the week and one of the things he wants from me is knowledge of what resources I need for the training department. Based upon what you know so far, do you think that I need to ask for a team of trainers to deliver all these different courses?" he asked.

"You are just one man, Phil. As you put together your plan for these learning events, you'll need to also think about where *you* need to be deployed, personally. It's no good you spending all your time in the training room with one business unit, and neglecting all the others. If it's anything like my world, you'll need to learn how to juggle many different requests from several business areas and that means utilising other resources."

"What are you saying, María? I'm not sure I understand; how do you 'juggle' things for your company? And what 'other resources' can I get?"

"Well, I look to prioritise my time to ensure I am spending it where the organisation can see their best returns. Right now, I would suggest that, for you, that is with the group that know and respect you the most, sales."

"But what about all the other business areas? They *all* need to be trained."

"For the other business units you'll need some help to deliver this training, because it is time critical for the company. In other words, when the company launch the new service in just a few months' time, you will need every business unit geared up and running with their new processes, knowledge levels and skills to execute. If I was you, I'd ask Gareth to sanction the use of trusted people from around the business to take on the delivery of the training. Maybe even some of the design too, because they are the subject matter experts."

"That makes sense María. I suppose the one thing that concerns me about that is that I am effectively washing my hands of what I would consider to be *my* responsibilities. I mean, *I* am supposed to be the training professional here, I shouldn't expect others to do my job for me!" he exclaimed in serious concern.

"Who said anything about absolving yourself of responsibility for that training? Certainly not!" she replied in mock indignation. "No, you will be responsible for ensuring that the training is to a high quality and that the delivery of their training hits a decent standard. That will probably involve you running your own 'training for trainers' course," María spoke with clarity and applied logic that Philip couldn't fault.

"Ah, I get it," he stated. "So, I need to work on the bigger picture and identify all the component parts of the training for the *whole* organisation. Then I can sub-contract out the design and delivery of each part that doesn't fall within my personal skill-set? I suppose too that, if I use internal staff and not supplier companies, it both cuts down costs for Woodroot Hosting, and also ensures that we have people around after the training that we can lean on for support during implementation?" Philip was lost in his thoughts, thinking out loud as he made notes on his pad, almost forgetting that he was on a call with María.

"Outstanding!" María's enthusiasm was clear to hear. "Not only have you got a commercially sound plan there to take to Gareth, but you have also thought about how the plan can be executed in the business units. Bueno, Phil."

"Oh, I was just thinking out loud María, but I'm glad it was along the right lines," Philip was beaming with pride, not that María could see though, and he was secretly rather pleased about that. "OK, I will have a think about how to structure training for each group and look to move into the 'design' stage. You're great María, thanks again, I owe you."

"Am I officially your 'mentor' now then Phil?" she replied with a chuckle.

"Would you mind?"

"It would be an honour. I'd love that." The words filled Philip with a warmth of comfort.

CHAPTER 7

DESIGN

Philip was in a cheerful mood. He was starting to see the wood for the trees now. He sipped his coffee as he finished drawing up his process map, as María had directed. Around all of the business units he drew a circle and inserted the corporate targets that the company was committed to achieve. Within the circle he listed the two measurable targets (as collected in discussions with the senior executives): revenue and employee engagement. Satisfied with this, Philip started to think that he needed to ensure that these corporate targets needed to be seen as the collective responsibility of ALL staff members, not just one group. He wondered whether there might be a need to design some form of 'universal' training event that everyone might receive to deal with matters that were appropriate to all staff. He elected to keep that in mind, and return to it later.

Turning his thoughts to the training, Philip drew lines on his diagram to section off each of the four main business units (sales, support, finance and HR). He decided that this looked 'about right' and that essentially there were four separate training events that he needed to think through and design, one for each group.

Finally, he asked himself a question and answered for each of the business unit training blocks on his diagram: *what do I want this group to do differently, once they have been trained?* Here, he listed down some key elements that he had compiled from his discussions with the business unit leaders.

Over the next couple of days, Philip built this list out with more detail. He took each of the business units in isolation and looked at the list of things he wanted the training to do for them, aligned of course to the discussions he had had in his 'research' phase. These, he thought, would form the basis of the training event for each unit. He prefixed each collection with the words *By the end of the training, the successful participant will:* and created each item as a unique objective. To help him, he had run an internet search on *how to write learning objectives* and discovered some great supporting material in the form of *Blooms Taxonomy*. What he particularly liked about the *Blooms Taxonomy: Teacher Planning Kit* was that it broke objectives down into low and high level 'thinking skills'. Low level skills included:

- Knowledge of
- Comprehension of

Whereas high level thinking skills were broken down into the following elements:

- Application
- Analysis
- Synthesis
- Evaluation

'Now I know what I want them to do differently' he thought to himself, 'next I need to think about what is the best vehicle to use to get the learning to them.' To help him in this, Philip decided to list down all the forms of delivery (of learning or information) he could think of. He knew that he may have missed some, but his list included:

- classroom
- e-learning
- webcast
- audio
- video
- self-study
- books
- qualifications
- coaching

After sending the list via email to María, she added a few more (some of which he knew he would need to research further to understand exactly what they were!):

- neuroscience
- gamification
- MOOCs (which he discovered stands for *massive open online courses*)
- social learning

Next, Philip thought about his audience and used his knowledge of the teams to figure out which training method might produce the most memorable form of learning experience for each business unit.

Looking through his list, he was beginning to feel more confident about his ability to do this job. It looked good. He had five training themes: one for all employees to frame the changes that were occurring in the organisation; the others specifically for each of the four business areas. Each theme was supported by several learning objectives and a suggested method of delivery.

With his document in front of him, Philip picked up the phone and dialed the now familiar number.

"María? Fancy meeting for lunch tomorrow? I think I am ready to hear what the next '*Disengaging Influence*' is."

CHAPTER 8

ABCD

"That's some really great work," María told Philip when she looked over his document. "You've got some solid foundations in place here for what will be 'memorable learning'."

"Thanks María, I appreciate you saying that," he replied, feeling a mixture of relief and pride. "I wouldn't have got this far without your help though. What I need to know now is what to do next with all of this?"

"Well, this is essentially what you are going to take to Gareth as your 'short-term' proposals, including the request to use some key people as seconded trainers from the business. You have the outline of your training sessions right here that you can share with that the secondees, but next, when you get them, you will need to figure out the content. Remember, each of the sessions will be different and therefore you, or they, are going to need to write different content for each. As you do that, keep the objectives you've written in front of you at all times. Be critical of the information you're putting into each session and ask yourself: *'if I tell them this, will it enable them to achieve the objectives, or is it surplus information?'* Be brutal in culling the content and filter out everything that isn't pertinent."

"Why do I need to do that?"

"We've all been to training where there has just been too much information thrown at us to remember anything; our brains just give up, saturated by facts and data. Make sure that you make it as simple as possible for the participant to remember what has been taught."

"How do I do that María? I'll bet you've got some tricks up your sleeve that will help me?" Philip enquired, jovially.

"Ha, ha. You bet I have!" she replied, confidently. "You know me so well already. Remember this one thing as we go this, Phil: *three is the magic number.*"

"Isn't that a song?" Philip chuckled.

"Ha ha. Yes it may be, but it's also the cornerstone of this model I'm going to give you. This model is based on the power of 'three'. The reason for that is that it has been proven that the maximum number of pieces of information we can remember effectively in any one sitting, is *three*. So you are going to need to look at the content and whittle the points down to a maximum of three key points. Let me give you an example. I was once asked to give a talk to the local youth group about swimming. My objective was to ensure that they learnt how to swim, encouraging them to learn if they couldn't already, or to swim safely if they were competent in the water to begin with. Firstly, I listed out anything and everything I could think of to do with swimming: from where to swim, through to what to wear when swimming; from the benefits of the exercise through to the dangers of swimming in certain places. I then condensed down my list to just three key points that I wanted them to walk away and remember:

1. The *benefits* of swimming
2. Where to swim *safely*
3. *How* to swim

"I now had the content material, but I needed to structure it into something that the audience would easily be able to follow, and this is where the 'ABC' structure comes in."

"You're having a laugh now, that's *another* song!" Philip interjected.

"Ha ha. Yes it is," she replied.

"I'm sorry María. Please continue, what is the 'ABC' structure? and is it as easy as '1-2-3'?" Philip laughed at his own joke.

"You know it?" María nodded with a cheery smile, aware that these acronyms would help Philip embed the knowledge she was sharing. "So, the ABC structure is going to help us order those three points whilst also ensuring that our audiences' attention span is maintained. You see, whenever I stand in front of a group of trainees, I know that there a number of questions flying around their heads and if I stand any chance of getting my point across to them, I'm going to need to answer those questions right up front. Once I have answered these questions, I know that they can concentrate on what I am here to deliver, do you see?"

"What questions?"

"Be patient, young Padawan!" María replied in a calm and slightly cheeky tone. "The ABC structure will help me answer these questions and not get sidetracked in the process. Between you and me, one of the worst things for a trainer to do is use up all their time telling them humourous and yet meaningless anecdotes that don't bear any relevance to key learning objectives."

As she was saying this, Philip's mind began to reflect back to his keynote speech at the conference. He suddenly felt himself colour up with subtle embarrassment. Philip knew that his presentation was almost entirely compiled of anecdotes, designed to amuse and entertain the audience rather than educate. When he recalled what feedback he received after the presentation, he realised it was entirely focused on his amusing delivery style and humour.

María continued, bringing his mind back to her.

"Imagine you are standing before a group of people you have never met before. Put yourself in the shoes of that audience for one moment. You'll probably be thinking either: '*I wonder what he is going to say now,*' or, '*this will be a waste of my time, but at least I can have a bit of a snooze while he talks*'. Perhaps you'll be deep in a conversation with the person you're sitting next to, or typing an important text on your phone. Either way, your first challenge is to gain the attention of your audience in a way that is going to spark their interest *and* be relevant to the subject."

"How?"

"You may start with an amusing anecdote, a quotation, or a joke. Some have started with a piece of music, a video or even some activity. I trained a group in the ABCD once, and gave them the homework overnight that they had to prepare an 'attention-grabber' for the following day. One of the group started his session juggling three compact cameras....and promptly allowed them to drop onto the concrete floor. As the cameras clattered to the ground, the audience gasped in horror - everyone's attention was fixed on the trainer by this time. The first words that he uttered were going to set the tone for the remainder of the session. We all breathed a sigh of relief when he eventually said: "*I want to talk to you today about the incredible durability of these little cameras because at some point, we are all going to drop them.*" Inspirational!"

"Wow, that sounds fun. So, the 'A' stands for ***Attention-grabber***?" asked Phil.

"Sí Phil, it does," María replied. "Be creative and have your own fun with it, it should only last for a couple of minutes at most."

"Does the 'B' stand for something too then?" he asked.

"Of course. The 'B' answers another one of those annoying little questions floating around the head of the audience. That question is: *why am I here?* Within a matter of seconds, you need to tell the group what they are going to gain from listening to you for however long the session is. 'B' therefore stands for..."

"***Benefits*** of listening!" interjected a very proud Phil, who felt as though he had just managed to get a cryptic clue from the newspaper crossword. "I like this game!"

"Yes! That's right. In the example of the cameras, the stated benefits of listening were: to understand how much punishment the camera could take before it would break."

"Cool," said Philip. "I think I can easily find the benefits from my list of objectives. What does the 'C' stand for?"

"Well, you have given me your attention, and you know how listening to me will benefit you, but you may well be questioning *my* ability to train you in the topic. I mean, you'll be thinking '*who are you to tell me about this, and why should I listen to YOU?*' The 'C' therefore stands for a **Credibility** *of the trainer* statement. You may not need to do this if you are already known to the group - it's really only for those occasions when you've not got a relationship with the group and need to show some authority."

"Do you mean like listing your qualifications?"

"It could be, but only if it is relevant to the topic you're training."

"So, alternatively it could be my experience in the field, for example?"

"Sí, precisely. In a few sentences, you need to outline what makes you an authority to talk to the group about this topic. When I was speaking to the youth group about swimming, my 'Credibility statement' was something like: '*My name is María. I was the regional champion in breaststroke and butterfly for 4 consecutive years in Madrid.*' Again, this shouldn't be a long, exhaustive biography or else it will distract the audience from your key message."

"I understand. It's easy to remember and keeps in the power of three!" stated Philip after a little reflection. "Besides which, I can see how a long '*Credibility*' statement may sound as though the session is going to be all about ME."

"Absolutely right."

They both sipped their coffee and took bites from their sandwiches. Philip finished making his notes from what María had just told him.

"There is a 'D' as well," María continued. "The 'D' is your statement of the **Direction** that this session is going to take. It again is in keeping with the magic number, 'three,' because in this statement you are going to signpost the *three* key points that you'll be talking about in detail through the session."

"What do you mean, María? Is this the main content of the course, or merely the headlines before we get into detail?"

"Good analogy Phil-these are just the headlines. It's like a newsreader who states what they are going to cover before they move into the main articles. In my swimming session, that was simply a case of me telling the group that: '*we are going to look at the benefits of swimming, where we can go to swim safely and how to get started if we can't swim*'. Again it's not a lengthy part of the session, but it answers the next one of the audience's questions: '*what's going to happen now?*'"

"Ah, *another* of their questions?" he smirked. "OK, so, we have done the ABCD of the session so far. How much time would have elapsed when doing this?"

"Not long at all. Probably no more than 5 minutes in total to be honest. Any longer than that and it's taking time away from the important information you need to get across to the group."

"5 minutes? Is that all? From the amount of preparation and effort involved in it, I thought it would be around 30 minutes!"

"I can see the logic there, but the first five minutes are arguably the most important of the session. They not only set the tone of it, but also give the audience a reason to continue to listen. If we lose their attention in the first five minutes, it's going to be a challenge to get it back; and we need their attention so we can get our message across. Also, if we lose them after five minutes, there's an even greater challenge ahead of us if we expect them to *recall* the learning at some point in the future."

"I can see that," Philip said. "OK, so what about the rest of the session?"

"Guess what? It follows the pattern of 'three'! Each of your three points will be tackled independently of the other, but broken down into a further three segments:

1. **Introduction** of the topic
2. The **details** of the topic
3. **Summary**

"You'll need to follow this same process for each of the three points you want to get across to the group. Once you've completed the final of the three points that you wanted to cover, you just need to build in a **conclusion**."

"Makes sense except one thing. Is there a difference between the '*summary*' and the '*conclusion*' in this model?" he asked, making copious notes.

"Sí, there is. The conclusion is simply the combined summaries from each of the three points that you'll have made. This helps the audience remember exactly what you've told them."

"Ah, I get that! So it *is* just like the presenter on the news. 'Tell 'em what you gonna tell 'em, then tell 'em, then tell 'em what you've told 'em," Philip joked.

"Yes, that's exactly right. That's the winning formula. The '*Conclusion*' is the final part of the design stage and can be supported by your training materials."

"Training materials?" Philip repeated slowly and in contemplation.

"Yes," replied María. "Once you've settled on the content, using this structure, you can then think about what the participants might need in order to reenforce or enhance their understanding. Sometimes this might be a visual aid like PowerPoint slides, handouts, workbooks, video clips you know, anything that is going to help you get your message across really."

"And do you use the same process or format for any type of training? I mean, does it work equally well for the classroom as it would for an e-learning piece?" he asked innocently.

"It does, Phil."

"Cool, I was once on a course that played a video about how to use consultative selling. It was hilarious. I wonder if it followed the format?" He spoke aloud, but this was a question he was posing to himself. María allowed for a further period of reflection for her student before continuing.

"If you are going to use any of these reenforcement methods, you'll need to think about the three ways that people like to receive information," María stated, refusing to get sidetracked into one of Philip's anecdotal stories that often turned out to be nothing more than a joke.

"Three AGAIN!" Philip said surprised.

"Yes, I suppose so!" replied María. "You see, when you communicate information to me, I can receive data from you in any or all of three ways: *Auditory*, you know, what I *hear*, *Visually* meaning information that I *see*-even you as you talk, and *Kinesthetically* through my sense of *touch*. It's sometimes known as the 'VAK' model. I may even prefer to receive information in one of these ways only. For example, when I was pitching to a potential customer, I noticed she had her eyes shut! It looked like she was blatantly trying to sleep as I talked and I thought that she was being extremely rude. Eventually I asked her if I was boring her. She immediately responded that she shuts her eyes in order that she can focus her entire attention on what I am actually saying, you know, the words I am using. Her preference was to receive information through her '*Auditory*' sense."

"Ah, so I guess things like slides and handouts are lost on people like that?"

"They can be," responded María. "But the trouble is, you don't know which sense your audience will respond to best. Instead, you'll need to ensure that you offer something for each sense."

"OK," said Phil. "Well, visuals are easy. Just throw up a few slides for them to look at..."

"No, it's not as easy as that Phil," María was quick to interject. "You see, your slides can *enhance* what you say, but can just as easily, they can *distract* from your message. In fact, *Visual* people can easily be distracted by what they see. Anything from what you wear, to your facial expressions, to the slides and the reactions of their fellow participants-all of these can distract them. And when you consider that it is anticipated most of us are highly sensitive to *Visual* data, like what people wear, body language, moving pictures etc, this is something we must take care to control."

"Right, so now I have two questions, I suppose. With regard to visual aids, are there any do's and don'ts you can share with me? And secondly, how can my appearance be used to good effect and not distract the group?" asked Phil credulously.

"These questions bring us to the next tier in the development of the training. After the period of design which, by the way, can take a long time, comes the *delivery* of the training. If we deliver training without proper preparation and thought, that's when we get poor quality training sessions and courses. I've seen a number of managers fall flat on their face thinking that they can deliver training: *"it's easy"*, they say. The fact is, it's easy to stand up in front of a group of people and talk, but it's actually a difficult skill to ensure that they *commit* what you say to memory."

"Is it?" Phil asked, with an element of shock. This was rocking his personal belief system as he knew that he was one of those who thought that training was just 'talking' to a group of people.

"No! That is just talking. Many managers that I come across reckon they can train. However, the reality is that these managers, I'm disappointed to say, are simply standing at the front of the classroom and just talking, and mainly to themselves."

"That sounds exactly like my school teachers!"

"Mine too," responded María who looked pensive for a moment. "I disliked my lessons at school for that reason."

"Me too!" stated Philip in surprise. "In fact, I was only just saying this to my Dad last time I saw him. I can't say that style of lecturing helped me learn very much at all."

"And that's the point, Phil. I'm not sure if they don't care if you learn or not, or if they lack awareness of whether their audience actually understand what they are saying? Maybe they are happily ignorant of whether the attendees can implement anything differently after the session? In fact, they are the ones that see training as a 'tick-in-the-box' exercise. Many training professionals refer to this attitude as 'sheep dipping' people through the training. You know, just ship them in and out of the course at speed. The irony is that often it's these same managers who are the first to complain that the people who've been trained haven't changed DESPITE being taken out of the workplace for the training!"

Philip sensed her frustration, but was not certain that her ideas would be cost effective. 'Sheep-dipping' (as she called it) seemed a pretty effective way of ensuring a large group of people were given the information quickly and at the same time.

"Maria, I see what you're saying, but surely those managers can lecture on what and how they need to change, or what they need to do their job properly? Particularly if they put it in an amusing way? The classroom just makes you able to communicate your message more efficiently to a larger group of people, surely?"

Maria was quick to retort. "But that is not *training* Phil, you can communicate to staff things that you want or need them to change, like a new process or an amended policy. That can be accomplished in a more appropriate setting, in, say, a team meeting or a 1:1. The point I am trying to impress upon you is that managers can misunderstand 'training' simply because they don't understand how people *learn*. What happens is that managers dump information on people and believe that their work is done. Training, they say, is something that they do TO people, not WITH them! Subsequently, they don't value our craft, because they haven't ever seen the fruits of it. They reckon training is a waste of time and that *everyone* only learns on the job. As we discussed before, this can be a valuable method, but is not always the most time or cost effective form of learning. The power of training is to educate *and* practice implementation in a 'safe environment'."

"You seem to be very passionate about this!" Phil said. He had seen a different side to María in this conversation. She had become fiery and passionate as she talked through her thoughts on the topic. He thought that she must have been hurt by some comments made about her training in the past and perhaps she still felt it was unjustified.

"I am," replied María, calming herself a little. "This is my profession that is being belittled by ignorant people. Training is a *skill*, it's not something that just any person can just pick up and be brilliant at. It takes time, experience and effort to be good. It's a skill that the vast majority of people will fail to achieve to a high standard, however."

"So how do I become one of those that trains to a high standard then María?" Philip quickly asked, attempting to move the conversation away from what was turning out to be a potentially bitter issue.

After a few minutes to compose herself, María asked: "Do you remember the diagram that I drew when we went to dinner?"

"Yes, in fact I have it here." Philip flicked through his notebook for the piece of paper she had given him.

"Great, let me add the next '*Disengaging Influence*' that causes training to fail," she said as she took the paper and wrote in the next segment:

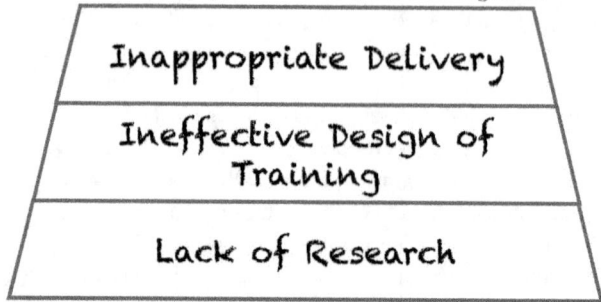

"**Inappropriate delivery**" Philip read out loud. "So, what exactly does that entail?"

"It's a broad question Phil and so I am going to have to give you a broad answer. When you deliver training there are so many variables, so many pitfalls, that can cause the participants to have a bad learning experience. The 'Design' phase of the training is to try to predict and mitigate these pitfalls, as best we can. Our job before the training even starts is to think about the environment we are training in. It's a training designer's responsibility to identify and alleviate the distractions before they even arise. We need to think about what the participants might see and hear *before* the session even starts. That is the point at which the '*Design*' phase of the training meets the '*Delivery*' part."

"Wow, that sounds a bit authoritarian," Philip stated with an alarmed expression.

María chuckled and shook her head. "It doesn't need to be, Phil. In fact, if you do it right, the group won't have a clue that you've put any thought or effort into it. They won't notice all the things that you've done prior to them entering the room; they will be completely unaware of the time and the thought you have put into everything prior to the session. They may even think that it's just 'happened' and it's right by accident!"

María laughed. It was the first time that Philip had seen her laugh properly before. Her eyes crinkled and she tossed her head back, her long black hair flowing obediently down her neck and resting on her shoulders. "I'm sure that's why so many people think that training is so easy and we are all a bunch of lazy wasters!"

Sensing that she was about to fall into another passionate rant, Philip decided that he needed to take action and move things along.

"Right, well now I want to know everything you do to create a truly *professional* standard of training delivery, María." Philip smiled a warm and encouraging smile.

"You have a winning personality, Phil. I can see why Gareth wanted you for this job; you can get people on your side using your charm. OK, I will tell you what I have found works well, but we are going to need the rest of the afternoon for this, so you'd better clear your diary."

CHAPTER 9

DELIVERY

"Take a blank sheet of paper. I'm going to ask you four questions and I want you to write down your brief responses; then we'll review them, ok?" María instructed.

"Check, I'm ready," said Philip with pen poised, hovering over his notepad expectantly. María continued:

1. "Think of the *worst* trainer you've ever had. What made him / her 'bad'?
2. "Think about the *best* training you've been to. What made it better than the rest?
3. "What training materials, you know, handouts, workbooks, slides etc. have you found useful *after* the training?"
4. "Describe the *worst* training room you've ever been in.

A moment or two of silence whilst Philip wrote was eventually broken.

"OK, I've got my answers to all of them."

"Bueno. What did you have for the your first answer relating to the worst trainer?"

"Er, well, there have been a few! I picked a fella called Ian that tried to train me on negotiation skills."

"OK, and what made him a 'bad' trainer?"

"He spoke on a monotone, was really boring. The topic was made to appear drab and disinteresting because of him. The content was uninspiring and I cannot recall a single thing he said!"

"Good lesson there then, Phil."

"How do you mean?"

"Your tone of voice is going to be important. Remember those that receive information best through listening? Well, they are sensitive to your tone of voice, your pitch, timbre and rhythm. It's not about the words here, it's about the *delivery* of those words. We'll come back to this later. What answer did you have for the second question about the *best* training?"

"Oh that one was easy. The best training I've experienced was when I was trained in people personality traits," enthused Philip.

"Oh that sounds interesting, what made it good?"

"It was an interesting subject of course, but the trainer, Warren, really made it live with some interesting anecdotes, jokes and exercises that really brought the message home. He was lively, enthusiastic and extremely personable. I remember he gave us all his contact details and asked us to write to him afterwards with stories of how we used our knowledge to good effect. I liked him a lot."

It was clear from his voice that Philip was remembering the experience with excitement, enthusiasm and easy of recall; a state that was not lost on María.

"Your enjoyment of this training is still alive in your memory today, Phil, and is clear through your voice tone. You seem to have a great recall of the content too. So what do you think we can learn from this experience?"

"I should imagine you're going to say that if you make the topic interesting, then you'll learn something?"

"Exactly, but there is more to it. If you can also present yourself as someone that the group can trust, someone who is there to help them improve, the group will open up to your information."

Philip nodded, sagely, as he contemplated this message.

"OK, so what about the materials? What have you found useful?"

"Easy one. None. I can honestly say I have never used anything that I have been given on a course. The exercises, files and books I have been give simply collect dust on my desk."

"That's a shame. Why weren't they useful for you?"

"Most of the handouts, files and books are cumbersome and not portable in the least. So when I was out in the field they weren't things I could take with me."

"Great point. So you might have found something a valuable aid to your memory if it could be carried around in your iPad case or even your wallet?"

"Yes, I think I would have. So long as it wasn't just a mass of words! Some of the diagrams might have been really useful to keep with me when seeing customers."

"Something else to remember when you design your supporting materials, Phil. Tell me about the *worst* training room you've ever been in then? What was it like?" María enquired.

"Oh, it was terrible," replied Philip. "There were no windows, it was dark and unwelcoming. The walls were bare except for a single whiteboard, without any pictures, it was just drab, horrible and depressing."

"And how did it make you feel being in there?"

Philip thought for a moment before responding. "I couldn't wait to get out. It felt almost claustrophobic."

"As a matter of interest, what did you learn on *that* course?" María asked.

Again, Philip gave it some thought, but after a few moments he gave up. "I can't remember, María! I think it was something to do with computer servers, but I'm not sure."

"That illustrates a good point Phil. I want you to remember that experience as a warning of how NOT to organise your training room. That room wasn't conducive to learning, it created a negative learning environment and guess what? You didn't learn anything, well, not that you can remember anyway. At the heart of it all, that's what we do, Phil: *memorable learning.* The training room is often totally overlooked by organisations, stuffed away in a cupboard or a soulless, windowless room somewhere. Before you even utter your first words, you are up against it, disadvantaged because of *where* you are delivering. If you have any say in your organisation about where to deliver the training, think about what makes for a pleasant environment that won't distract the people. You want them to feel comfortable so that their minds can focus and concentrate on what is important: your message."

"What size of room works best, do you think? If I have a choice, that is," Philip asked.

"It depends on the size of the group that you're training Phil," she responded. "If, for example, you're training a small group of five people, you don't want to be in a huge room that can hold 50 because that will make them feel uncomfortable, rattling around in a big space. Equally, rooms that are too small for the group size don't work either, as people will invariably feel too uncomfortable, overlooked and too 'claustrophobic', as you called it, to learn."

"That doesn't really answer my question María!" stated Philip slightly tetchy.

"Are you asking what size GROUP works best for training? rather than the size of the *room*?" retorted María assertively.

"I suppose I am," he replied, a little sheepishly.

"Well, the optimum size for learning is said to be twelve, Phil. I've worked with both larger and smaller groups, but I have also found 12 to be a pretty good size. When I was trained as a trainer, they stated that Jesus obviously knew his stuff because he took *twelve* disciples to train!" María stated, flashing Philip a smile that he momentarily lost himself in. They both looked into each others eyes for a moment longer than was comfortable, then pulled away with an embarrassed jerk.

Eventually, after what felt like an age, Philip asked: "So, let's say that there is a group of twelve, how would you organise the tables and chairs for maximum impact and learning potential?"

"That's a really professional question to ask," María responded. "And one that needs to be considered in connection to the TYPE of training that you are giving."

María took Philip's notebook and found a fresh page of paper to draw on. On it she drew several diagrams labelled with numbers. "The circles are your participants, Phil," she explained. "And the rectangles are their work tables. Tell me, which layout do you think would work best for you if you were just briefing the group on something, not anticipating a 2-way conversation with the group?"

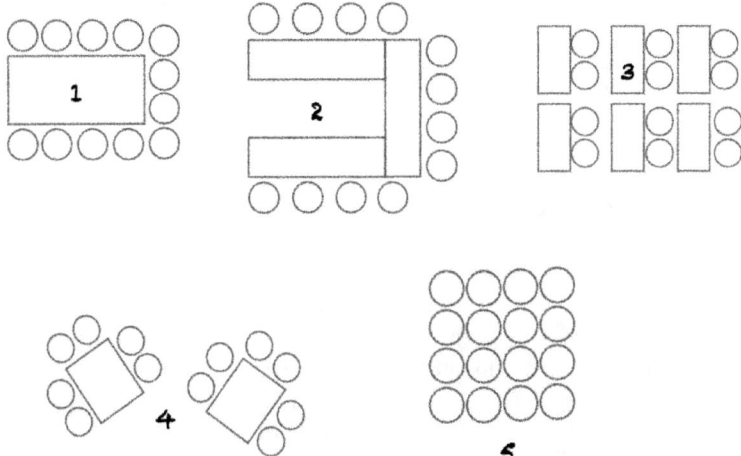

Philip took the notebook and studied it for a short while. "My first reaction, if I am honest with you María, was to say 'All of them!' But then I got to visualising briefing the group in each layout. So I am going to say that the *most* conducive one for a one-way communication, like a presentation, would be number 5."

"Awesome!" enthused María. "The way you approached that question was precisely the right way to do it. Put yourself in the shoes of the listener and identify what *they* need in order to receive the message. Now tell me why you selected number 5, why was it better than the others?"

"Well, I think that this layout is like a conference and I simply thought: 'At a conference, the speaker delivers a message with little or no interaction with the audience', so that seemed like the right choice," he responded.

"Spot on! I like the way you think," said María encouragingly, flashing another winning smile. "The layout is designed so that *all* the attention is focused on the speaker, and none on the individual participants. This means that if the speaker was to ask the audience for questions, or to respond to one of their questions, the group would need to be turning themselves around in their seats in order to see who answered it."

"If that happens too much, I guess we could find an audience suing us with neck muscle strains!" joked Philip, feeling truly comfortable now in María's company.

"Ha ha. I guess that's possible," she laughed. For the first time, María seemed to notice that Philip had a really warm, friendly smile. "The group are going to learn most by sitting in a comfortable position, and this means facing in the direction of the speaker, whoever that is. There is another issue relating to this layout that could create an obstacle to learning, any idea what it is?"

"Let me see now," Philip thought for a moment. "Is it anything to do with the lack of tables for them to write on? That seems like the most obvious difference between this diagram and the others."

"Kind of," responded María. "Tables are useful to rest note books on to write comfortably, that's true. But they also create boundaries for our personal space. They establish kind of borders that say: 'this area is for me, that area is for you.' As strange as this may sound, having that space to call your own, can help the individual relax and therefore absorb your message."

"So, conversely, *not* having that space is going to be a distraction, or at least prevent the group from learning?" he asked.

"It can do. It depends on how long you are going to keep them in the room like that."

"That makes sense. I'm thinking that this is only any good for a short session of, say, an hour?" Philip stated, his tone of voice was asking for her approval.

"I'd say that would be the longest you would want to have a session in a room layout like this Phil. OK, so let's say that you have a *one day* training event and you have a lot of information to share with the group, but you also want them to ask questions and share experiences with each other. Which layout would you choose for this?" María asked with a wry smile.

Philip's mind was sent spinning. He looked through each of the diagrams finding reasons for and against their use. After what seemed like an hour, but was probably only a minute, Philip let out a long sigh and answered: "I think number '4', because having a group on each of the tables means that they can discuss things between themselves pretty effectively like that."

"Yes, they can. Why did you deliberate so long before deciding on that answer?" María asked, feeling that there was more to Philip's response which needed to be teased out of him.

"Because I looked at number '2' and felt that there could be some good discussions across the room that way too."

"So why did you not choose number '2'?" María asked with a mock tease in her voice.

"Hmmmm, I don't know, now you've put me on the spot! What is the right answer?"

"So, you are right that layout number '4' will produce some good group discussions because they are all around the same table. That is why this style is going to work best when your training has a lot of group work, exercises, discussions and you may even introduce the element of competition between the tables."

"I was right then!" Philip stated triumphantly throwing his hands up in the air in mock celebration.

"No!" responded María in a sharp tone as if to mock his premature celebration. "You see, layout number '2' is the better one for the task that I set you. Do you remember what sort of training I said was going to be conducted?"

"Er, I thought you said it was training where you wanted some discussion?" Philip replied a little hurt, his ego slightly bruised. He had always been a highly competitive individual that loved to win at anything and that is why he always had felt well-suited to sales.

"I said that, but I *also* stated that the training involved a lot of information that you, as the trainer, would need to deliver. On this basis, you will need to fix people's attentions on you, or on a screen. Option '2' gives you the ability to do this because you can stand in a place that everyone can see both you *and* the screen; or you can walk up the centre of the 'u' and chat to individuals. In fact, this format is by far the most popular one for a lot of trainers because they find that they can control the group most effectively with it."

"What do you mean 'control the group' through this layout?" enquired Philip, his natural interest again peaked.

"When I first moved into training, I was really lucky because I was put on a training project with an external training consultant called Sylvia. Sylvia made it her mission to teach me everything she knew and lot of what I am telling you now is because she had the patience to help me understand what I should do in the role. She sat me down one day and asked me: 'Have you ever thought about 'seating psychology'? She may as well have asked me what the square route of some 16-digit number was! So she drew me out the same picture that I have drawn here, in figure '2', and proceeded to tell me what to expect from the people that sat in each position around the 'u' shape."

"That sounds heavy!" Philip said, aghast that this training malarky was becoming so psychological and not at all how Gareth had sold it to him.

"Not really," María retorted. "Not when you listen to this and test it in your training sessions. It's really just common sense, mixed with a bit of knowledge through experience."

"OK, so what did she say?" Philip asked with an air of skepticism now.

María went to take Philip's notebook that she had drawn in, but as she did so her hand gently brushed Philip's. Sensing this, he glanced at her face and was sure that he saw her cheeks slightly flushed for a moment. As she talked, she wrote against each of the place positions in the diagram labelled '2'.

"Firstly," she started, a slight waver in her usually confident voice. "I want you to remember a golden rule. The psychology of seating *only* works for the first people that come into the room, because *they* have a choice over where they can sit. For those that take their places later, what I'm about to tell you is irrelevant because they had no choice where to sit. Those that have the choice will sub-consciously select the place that they *feel* is right. This feeling may be the result of their mood that they are in that day, but it may equally be a reflection of how they feel about the topic of the training- or even you, personally!"

"Now I'm intrigued. Tell me more?"

"OK, so, assuming that they have no disability, like poor eyesight or difficult hearing, and they sit right here," María pointed at the two positions on either side, and at the very ends of the 'u'. Philip's eyes fell along her slim, well manicured finger. "These places are for your 'learners'. Those who select these seats are the ones that have come to learn, and therefore want to support you because you are the one through whom they will 'learn'. It's possible that they even have some knowledge on the topic already, to a certain degree anyway, and may want everyone in the room to know it, including you. They have an element of expertise and want to show it off, but by the same token want to learn from the 'expert', the 'guru'. If you don't prove yourself to be their guru, then they may become withdrawn from the group and disengaged or even try to take over."

María wrote '*initially keen **learners** - may think themselves experts*' against this position on the diagram.

"Then we have these two in the middle of each long side," she said as she indicated the places with her pen. "They are the ones that position themselves with the others in the class surrounding them for maximum protection. They want the feeling of 'security' that comes when they are surrounded by allies, but also they like the notion that they can 'hide' from you. They are effectively 'hiding' behind those closer to the front."

"Hide?" Philip repeated.

"Yes. They can physically duck behind the 'learners' and break eye contact with you if you stand at the front, in the hope that you won't ask them questions or make them speak to the rest of the group. They are *potentially* good learners, but will need your *encouragement* to join in with group discussions and share their experiences. So, when they enter the room, they are what I call the '*blank pages*'."

"Blank pages? What on earth..?" laughed Philip.

"Yeah. Their role in the group has not yet been written and you have the opportunity to bring them onside with you, or you can lose them just as easily. They can be moulded. How you work with them is going to dictate whether they are committed to learning, or remain unparticipative and neutral. You'll need to build their confidence perhaps, or encourage them when they speak to offer more. Either way, if you leave them alone, they will intellectually drift away and you stand a good chance they won't learn from your session."

"Wow, so much to think about and remember!"

"It's not as easy as you thought, is it? Watch out for these ones in the corner too, Phil. They are likely to be the most reluctant people in the room to get involved. This is the position which is best for anyone who wants to 'hide' from your eye contact, and therefore not participate in the training at all. They may be the silent skeptics that have preconceptions before entering the room about this training, but equally don't want to share it with you or anyone else."

"Goodness! This is beginning to sound like a load of land mines waiting for me to step on!" said Philip, astonished at just how complex this job was beginning to feel.

"In a way it is. If you don't do your homework and know where to place your efforts in the room, you'll only speak to a couple of the group and lose the rest of the participants. The good news, though, is that if you get it right, your training will be a massive hit," María stated with a smile.

"I've got a hundred things running around my head now María, but what about the top row? You haven't told me about them yet," asked Philip, slightly dazed.

"Sí. This is the row to tread very carefully with in the session, Phil," started María, gravely.

"What? and the others aren't?!" exclaimed Philip in disbelief.

"Not by comparison! These two here," she pointed to the two at the corners of the back line. "Have the same sentiment as the others that park themselves in the corners, but these," she tapped her finger on the two places immediately centre of the four along the base of the 'u'. "They are the two that I call the '*would-be dominators*'. They have potentially come to the training in opposition, in protest or to complain about you or the topic. Maybe they are dissatisfied with the direction the company is taking or think that they don't need this training. Perhaps they feel that their time would be better spent out in the field making money, or back at their desk fixing issues. Either way, your work is cut out with these people."

As Philip reflected upon María's words, he thought back to his own experiences in the training room as a student. He was embarrassed to recall the number of times he had sat in these places with that exact same notion, believing that his time would be better spent out there, selling. He felt slightly ashamed of himself now that he was on the inside, looking out at the group.

"So," María continued. "You'll have a seating arrangement looking something like this." She turned the notepad around and showed Philip what she had written beside each placement.

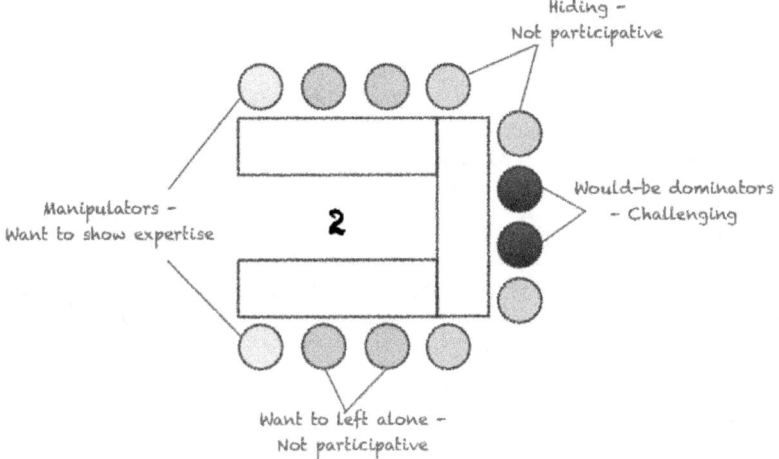

Philip looked at her neat handwriting and sub-consciously made the comparison with his own spidery style. Her handwriting was lovely, thoughtful and clear. He felt that maybe her handwriting reflected her mind.

"Thanks María, you are wonderful, and so good to me. I truly appreciate the time you're taking to help me...and stop me from looking a right idiot!" As Philip said this, and he realised he meant every word. He was beginning to appreciate that training was far from easy, and was certainly more than Gareth had indicated to him when he asked him to take the job. He now acknowledged that training was not simply about turning up to any old room and presenting, but there was, in fact, a science behind everything. A science that could help people learn, and not forget.

"So, what about layout numbers '1' and '3'?" he asked, "When would I use those?"

"What does number '3' look like to you?" she asked.

"Well, it reminds me of my school days!" Philip replied in jest.

"Exactly!" María said emphatically.

Waiting for an explanation that didn't seem to be forthcoming, Philip stated "I don't understand. So, is it a layout that is redundant for anything outside of a school classroom?"

"Not at all" María replied. "Our technical instructors seem to prefer this type of layout for their sessions because they are at the front demonstrating the keystrokes where all can see. The participants can then replicate the same keystrokes at their desks without having to change position or even move their heads. Here's a question for you, Phil: if you, as the technical trainer, want to observe what the participant is doing on their screens, how would you organise the desks and monitors?"

"Man, you ask some really tough questions María! Up until about half an hour ago, I wouldn't have thought to change the room to any specific layout, let alone think which is the best to observe participant monitors!"

He thought for a moment and as he did so, María found herself willing him to get the right answer and continue the impressive roll that he was on.

"Er....well, this is going to sound weird," Philip eventually responded. "But, I think I might go for an 'inverted u-shape' with the participants on the *inside* of the 'u' rather than sitting on the outside. That way their screens are facing me as I walk in the middle of the 'u'. I also think that if I wanted their attention I could ask them to face me and that way their backs will be to their screens. Then they won't get distracted or tempted to play on the internet as I speak!"

"Phil, you are outstanding! That's precisely what I have found works best for that type of training. Wow, you are so impressive, a natural, perhaps!" María flashed him a smile that filled Philip with another warm glow of pride. "OK, last layout then. What does number '1' remind you of?"

"Now this one I am struggling with," replied Philip. "Because this one just looks like a load of people around a single table, just like any old meeting. In fact, this is how I held my training session the other day because it was in a meeting room."

Philip was clearly challenged with this one and was going to need a little help to identify how he might use this particular layout.

Eventually, she asked: "If it *was* a meeting, why has this layout become the normality for meetings nowadays? What does it encourage?"

"I suppose everyone can see everyone else, so it encourages open discussion? But I don't see how that works for *training*?" Philip stated, confused.

"Not *all* training will necessitate *you* to be the focus of attention, Phil," María replied with a chuckle. "There will be occasions when the participants will learn from each other, and that requires them to discuss things openly as a group. In those circumstances, your role is that of a chairperson to nurture the discussion and move it in the right direction. So, this layout can be really useful for things like team-bonding sessions when you want the group to work together, or open up to each other about how they think or feel. Does all this make sense?" María asked, now nervous that she had over-loaded him with information.

"It does," he said ponderously. "But there is so much to consider and think about. I am utterly amazed at the science behind what you do, María; and just how much you have to think about, even before the session starts. I don't know I will ever be able to remember all of this."

Something deep within Philip was now starting to stir, was it a nervousness or perhaps even a fear that he was going to fail at this role. He had never failed in anything he had done before. This was completely alien to him. Maybe this was this going to be the first time he had shown himself incapable of achieving a high standard of something? Self-doubt was beginning to rise up in his heart and he hated to feel this way.

Sensing that Philip was beginning to feel out of his depth, María decided that she needed to broaden out his support mechanism and find others that may be able to help.

"Phil, one of my trainers is doing a session next week. If you can free up your diary, do you fancy coming over to the training centre to observe? I can brief him on why you'll be there, and he can take you through what he is doing, and what his thought processes are, all in 'real time'? You might find it useful."

"Oh, if that is ok, that would be brilliant," replied Philip with an element of relief. He felt he was being afforded the opportunity to associate theory with reality each time María suggested some plan of action. "I can free up the whole day. It would be great to see all this in action."

"Will you do me a favour then?" María asked.

"Of course, anything," he replied eagerly. A little *too* eagerly perhaps, he then reflected.

"Once the day has finished, will you provide me with some feedback on Eddie, the trainer? I would love to get your thoughts on his style of delivery and how well he manages the group through the process of learning."

"Of course I will, María," Philip's enthusiasm was clear. "In fact, I will go one better than that. To say 'thank you' for everything you have done for me so far, I am going to take you out to dinner at that new restaurant that has just opened up downtown...if you don't have any plans that is?"

With a sudden realisation of what he had just done, Philip felt embarrassed and as though he had just over-stepped the invisible lines of 'professionalism'. Self-doubt again arose like a sea dragon from the deep; had he made a fool of himself and over-stepped the mark by asking her out? He hated the notion that this might be taken as a romantic suggestion, rather than a heart-felt 'thank you'. He wished he hadn't asked and risked ruining their perfectly functional, working relationship. What a fool he was.

"That sounds very kind of you Phil, muchos gracias. I will ensure I am free," she replied in a professional manner, smiling and looking into Philip's eyes. If she had thought he was asking her on a date, she didn't let it show at all.

Philip breathed a sigh of relief as they parted with their usual goodbyes. It was then that he caught himself noticing how beautiful her brown eyes were, and just how much he enjoyed being around her.

CHAPTER 10

IN ACTION

"Good morning, you must be Philip? I'm Eddie. It's terrific to meet you."

Eddie greeted Philip in the reception with a warm handshake, strong eye contact and a beaming smile that immediately put Philip at ease. A middle-aged man with a greying beard and no hair on his head at all, Eddie seemed exuberant and content with life.

"María has told me a little bit about you," he said. "I'm happy to help, but tell me, what are *you* hoping to get out of our day together?"

"I'd just like to get a feel for how a professional trainer thinks, and what decisions you make during the day," replied Philip. "If that works for you?"

"Of course," Eddie maintained his smile as he spoke. "I'm going to introduce you to the group before we start this morning. I shall just tell them that you are observing ME since you are moving into training and want to gain some ideas. Is that ok?"

"Perfect Eddie, thanks." Philip already felt himself warming to the man, though he couldn't put his finger on what Eddie had done to facilitate that.

The pair then made their way to the canteen to collect a coffee before the session started. Eddie took this opportunity to bring Philip up to date on the training schedule for the day, along with the message he was attempting to ensure all attendees remembered.

"Can I ask you a question Eddie?" Philip asked afterwards. "I understand what this session is trying to achieve, but why is it being run in the first place? What is the business need that has been identified?"

"Good question Philip. Information I should have started with, sorry. The reason for this training is because our company is being acquired. We are getting bought out by a larger organisation and there is a great deal of speculation, confusion and unrest amongst the staff. They are concerned for their jobs, fearful of the change that is about to happen. The managers that I am about to train will need to help their team through a massive period of change over the next few months. My role is to support them in that."

"Goodness," exclaimed Philip. "I had no idea that was happening! I've known the owners for years too. Are there going to be any redundancies? Will all employees keep their jobs?"

"I'm anticipating this will be one of the first questions we will need to review in the course today. The answer is that it's likely that there will be some casualties, yes," replied Eddie gravely. "We don't yet know the full impact of the acquisition yet, but there is a good chance that some people will be made redundant, so I need to help the managers prepare for all eventualities."

"Where does that leave you...and María?" Philip asked, concern in his voice.

"We are in the mix along with everyone else, I suppose," Eddie replied, his tone was very matter-of-fact. Philip considered how difficult this training might be for Eddie under such ambiguous circumstances.

"How do you feel about it all? Isn't it difficult to train with *that* hanging over your head?"

"Not really," Eddie responded a little sharply. "When I go into the training room, I focus on the job I have to do, and I will do it to the best of my ability, irrespective of what is happening in *my* 'world'. You see, I believe that this is what it takes to be a 'professional', Phil. You cannot bring your personal troubles into an environment where people are trying to learn. It's a sure-fire way of distracting them from the learning. As soon as I train the group, I go into a kind of 'performance-mode'."

"A performance? Do you mean like an actor?"

"Exactly like an actor. They don't take their personal troubles onto the set or stage, but embrace their role in a professional manner, at least until the lights go down and the curtains close. The training room is my stage, Phil, and the participants are my audience."

"Interesting perspective Eddie. I can understand what you're saying and it makes perfect sense. I suppose that if you allow personal feelings into your session, you will become inconsistent and open yourself up for criticism," Philip mused. "But, are you saying that if this is a 'performance' that a trainer is a form of 'entertainer'?" In his head, he was recounting the words that Gareth had said to him when he was offered the job.

"Absolutely and categorically NOT!" replied Eddie emphatically. "Many trainers have received great accolades because they 'entertain' the participants. They are said to be 'funny', 'entertaining' or 'amusing' and they may even have people queuing up to get on their courses. They are the types that measure their success in terms of numbers of people trained, you know, 'bums on seats'."

"But surely that's a good indicator of success?" Philip questioned.

"If they were in the entertainment industry that would certainly be true, Phil. But *we* aren't. We are in the *learning* industry and that means that our participants come to us in order to *learn* something new, something they didn't know before they came into the room. Learning requires the ability to remember. Storing the information in their brain so that they can use it again when they go back to their desks or out into the field. There is no doubt that these 'entertainers' provide an 'enjoyable' experience, but the problem is that the jokes become the focus of the training and the learning gets pushed into the background. I have no problem with jokes in the training room. Humour, used well, is actually a very effective tool for participant engagement, the point is that it needs to be used as a tool to *enhance* already well developed and delivered training, not be the focus."

"I get your point Eddie."

Eddie didn't seem to register Philip's words as he continued. This was clearly a passionate topic of his. "I've asked participants a couple of months after the training event what they learnt from this type of training, and all they could recall were some amusing anecdotes or jokes! Very little of what they remembered was of any use to them in their jobs, but they all said they would go to that person's training again."

"Why?" asked Philip, flabbergasted. It made no sense to him; why would anyone want to go to a learning event knowing they wouldn't learn anything?

"Simply for fun and amusement," Eddie responded. "Certainly not to learn! All they would get out of a session like that would just be the enjoyment of a 'show', not any knowledge or skill, probably. This type of trainer tends to be very egoistic, I have found. They want the accolades from the audience, just like an actor on the stage. They love the recognition that they get from the audience, the verbal applause."

"I see." Philip was deep in thought. He was thinking of his own experience with a trainer whose events he had attended several times, Poonam. He found himself trying to recall what he had learnt from her. He had always considered her to be the most entertaining trainer he had ever encountered. In the end, he gave up and had to agree with what Eddie was saying, but one thing was nagging away at him and he just had to ask: "Are you saying that all training should be dull and unentertaining, like a Victorian school classroom?"

"Ha ha. No! I would never condone that," Eddie replied with a chuckle. "I subscribe to the belief that a trainer should be almost anonymous."

"OK. Now I am intrigued. What do you mean, anonymous?" Philip asked eagerly.

"If you think about it, a trainer should never be the centre of attention for the group, unless they are delivering information. You see, it's not all about me, as a trainer, it's about the participants learning what we deliver to them. My job is not to entertain, but if I manage to do that whilst the group learn what I say, my objective is still achieved. You see Phil, my role is to *facilitate* their learning in whatever way possible and make it a 'memorable' experience."

"Ah, María has used the terms 'facilitator' and 'trainer' in the context of training before. Are they one of the same, or two different roles?" Philip enquired.

"They are very, very different," Eddie stated emphatically. "A trainer is someone that can educate the learner through a mixture of teaching information, exercises and tests; whereas I look at a *facilitator* as more of a 'classroom coach'. A facilitator has to tease information and experiences out of the participants in order to make their point. They are skilled in the art of questioning, listening *and* summarising more than simply 'informing'."

"I see, Eddie. And which are you?"

"I have to be both, Phil."

Eddie's response shocked Philip. He was expecting him to answer one or the other. He had to ask: "How do you mean, Eddie?"

"There are some occasions when I need to be a trainer and teach people some things like product information, new processes and so on. At most other times I need to be a facilitator though, because I believe that people come to a better understanding of something when I *help* them understand, not tell them. I subscribe to the little saying that if I *tell* them something, they can take it or leave it, but if *they* tell me something, well, that's because they believe it. I reckon they must have made the mental connections in their brain already, and that's what helps the memory process, isn't it?"

Philip wondered whether this was the issue that María wanted his feedback on. Perhaps she was looking to him to give his observations on whether Eddie was a 'trainer' or a 'facilitator'. He made a mental note to watch Eddie's style closely and assess which role he took in this session.

As they entered the training room, Philip made a study of the environment. The first thing he spotted was probably the first thing participants would be confronted with: a sign on the door that clearly stated what training was happening in the room and who their trainer was. 'No surprises for anyone entering the room,' he thought to himself, 'I like that.' He speculated there would be no confused delegates, opening training room doors and asking which room their training was in; he made a mental note to introduce this at Woodroot.

The next thing he noticed was how the tables were arranged. Eddie had gone for the traditional 'u' shape with the seats on the outside and Philip immediately recalled his conversations with María about that.

Arranged in front of each chair on the desk was a note pad, pen and a workbook. One thing that Philip made a note to ask Eddie about later, was the absence of name plates by each place. The training that Philip had attended in the past had always had the obligatory name plate against each seat and he wondered whether Eddie had simply forgotten to lay them out.

Taking his place at the back of the room, Philip set himself up with his notebook and felt his cell phone vibrate in his pocket. He had a text from María:

Have a great day with Eddie today. REALLY looking forward to our dinner tonight :-). Oh, look out for Eddie's little trick as people come into the room!x

Philip smiled at the message, his eyes focussing on the addition of an 'x' at the end. Did that mean anything? or did she do that to everyone?

Suddenly aware that people were arriving in the room, Philip's thoughts returned to observing Eddie. As each delegate entered the training room he noticed that he greeted them by shaking their hand and introducing himself to them. After about the third person, Philip felt that Eddie was maintaining eye contact with the participant a little longer than was 'normal'. Normal to him, that was. He wondered whether this was a conscious thing that Eddie was doing; he certainly looked intensely into their eyes as he shook their hands.

Conversations amongst the group were burbling until Eddie stood in the centre of the tables, waited for a moment until the room fell silent and then stated in a loud voice: "If nothing in this world ever changed, there would be no butterflies."

Then after a few seconds pause, he continued. "Together we are going to discover how to make the process of change as painless as possible for our teams. We will understand how humans react and cope with the process of change."

Eddie moved to a different spot at the centre of the group.

"Thank you for your punctuality this morning, it's greatly appreciated because we have a lot to cover today, including a look at the Kubler-Ross change curve, what that means to our team members, plus the skills *we* need to employ to help them get to a place where they can accept change. Finally, we will look at how quickly, or slowly, we can expect people to get to the point where they think positively about change."

Upon hearing this, Philip flicked back a few pages in his notebook to one of the first conversations he had with María about designing a session. Sure enough, he thought, Eddie has already followed the 'ABCD' of the session, though he missed out the 'C' and Philip wondered why. Something else to ask Eddie in the break.

After going through the agenda for the day, Eddie introduced the obligatory "getting to know you" piece. As a participant, Philip hated this part. It was always uncomfortable to be waiting for your turn to come around, waiting till the finger of doom pointed at you, like a hand moving around the clock face. He remembered what it was like, knowing your turn was coming, getting ever closer with each person around the table. He recalled that this was a source of ever increasing nervousness, and worse for many of his colleagues Philip that attended the trained with. However, Eddie shocked him.

He invited all the managers to stand up and come into the centre of the room. Then he asked them to go around and introduce themselves to each other and chat for a short while. There was an initial awkwardness, but after a while the participants overcame their reluctance and the room was filled with chatter and noise. After a few minutes, Eddie asked everyone to return to their places.

Eddie then stated: "Helping individuals cope with change demands that we first know the person, the individual we are wanting to change, as we are going to find soon. So, by way of getting to know each of us we are going to have a little exercise."

Philip was pleasantly surprised that Eddie did not invite each participant to prepare a list of interesting facts about themselves, as he had been forced to do on many training courses before. Instead, he asked them to get a fresh sheet of paper and write the numbers 1 through 12 in a column. Next he stated that he had spoken to each of their teams in preparation for the training, and they had all told him an interesting fact about their manager. Eddie was going to read out this fact and the participants were to write down which person around the room it referred to.

The subsequent buzz in the room was noticeable and Philip felt the energy levels surge with excitement and competition.

Furthermore, Eddie seemed to know the name of every person around the room as he read out the correct answers. Philip concluded that he must know each of these participants and have trained them before. 'Impressive though,' assessed Philip.

BREAK

"I've got a few questions to ask you Eddie, is that ok?" Philip asked when the last of the participants had left the room in search of coffee.

"No worries," replied Eddie with a smile. He had clearly expected to field a number throughout the day.

"At first I thought that you had neglected to put out name plates for the session today, but after the first session, it was clear that you didn't because you already knew all of the participants..."

"Why do you assume that, Phil? I've never met them before, actually!" Eddie interjected.

"But you seemed to know everyone by name when you were doing the opening 'getting to know you exercise'! You seriously didn't know them?"

"Not before they entered the training room, no," he stated emphatically. Philip was beginning to appreciate that there were no half-measures with Eddie. "I knew their names from the participant list, but I have never met them before."

"How on earth did you get *all* their names right first time then?" questioned Philip in amazement.

"Ah, that's a little trick I learned when I was on a course once. It's all to do with facial association. I make a point of introducing myself to everyone that comes into the room. As they tell me their names, I look at their faces and associate their names to something, so that way, I can remember them."

"I'm not sure I understand what you mean."

"OK, well let's take Russell as an example. When Russell introduced himself, I looked at his face and superimposed on it a mental picture of my Jack Russell dog. That way, when I looked at him in the session, I remembered my dog and my brain associated him with the name 'Russell'!" Eddie stated proudly.

"Good job it didn't flash up the name Jack!" Philip joked as they both chuckled. "And you did something like that for all of the participants?"

"Yes, it's amazing what the brain can recall when it's associated with pictures."

"Cool. I found that really impressive. My other question was around the structure of the session. I guess you work to the 'ABCD' set up?"

"Yes, María taught me that when I first came here, it's great." Eddie wondered whether that was the question or if there was more.

"I thought as much," said Philip with a smile. "But you left out the 'C' part. You didn't mention your credentials and I wondered why that was the case?"

"Oh, good spot!" Eddie was impressed. "That's because the 'credentials' part is not always necessary. If I was to train the group on something that I had discovered, something new that would radically change their perceptions, then maybe I could have stated my credentials at the opening. I am training them on things that are in the public domain already and have been for many years. All I am doing in guiding them through the information that they could access themselves, if they had the time. I took the decision that giving my 'credentials' wouldn't be of any benefit to the session, so left it out."

"Ah, I'm glad I asked. I think I might have fallen into the trap of inserting *credentials* into every session!" he declared honestly.

"We need to get back to the room Phil, the break is nearly over; but before we return I wanted to give you the 'heads up' about the dynamics in the room...or have you already spotted our characters?"

"I'm sorry Eddie, I don't know what you mean," replied Philip honestly.

"Has María taken you through the 'Psychology of seating' as she calls it?" Philip nodded. "OK, well Tanya, that's the one sitting directly opposite me on the back row, has already shown she is not happy to be here. Her body language is negative, her tone of voice is clipped and aggressive. Have you noticed how many times she has disagreed with me already this morning?" Eddie enquired.

"No, I'm sorry, I hadn't picked up on any of that!" Philip was genuinely surprised that this had been going on without his awareness. He resolved to watch the participants more closely for the remainder of the morning.

"Watch out, too, for the chap sitting at the front on my left, James. He has been here for a long time and has probably attended every training that has ever been offered, but that seems to have left him believing that he knows everything. He has tried to take over the session on a couple of occasions already. He has acted as if *he* is the trainer. I will need to try to control both of them."

"I hadn't noticed that either! I thought James was just trying to get involved and support you actually, but now you come to mention it, he hasn't really helped you move the session forward, perhaps."

"No, he hasn't. I've taken the liberty of printing out the slides that I'm going to use in this next session, Phil. That will help you see what I am trying to cover, so you'll know what information I'm training the group."

Eddie handed over three pages, each of which had several miniature slides printed on them. Philip wondered why he had been given these *before* the session. Surely, Philip thought, he could simply read them when they came up on the screen?

Philip returned to the training room and resumed his position at the back of it just as another text vibrated his cell phone. It was María once more:

Hola Phil, how is it going? I hope you're making notes on Eddie's delivery style to chat with me later. Did you spot his trick with the names of the participants?x

Philip quickly typed his response:

Hi María. This is a great learning experience for me. I owe you...again. Yes, I can't wait to have a go at this 'name association' thing Eddie does! xx

After he pressed 'send', he realised that he had put two 'x's on the end of his message. Once again, his doubts and concerns flooded through his mind - would María read something into that, or would she simply see it as a response to hers?

'Oh well,' he thought, 'nothing I can do about it now. I shall just have to focus on the session and deal with any fall out later.'

LUNCH

At lunch, as they sat over a sandwich, Philip and Eddie chatted over the morning session. Philip was appreciative of the opportunity to learn from someone that has clearly learnt how to deal with the diversity of people in a training room.

"I see what you mean about James and Tanya," he opened. "When Tanya questioned why you were asking them to do the last exercise, I wondered whether she was going to tell you she wouldn't do it!"

"Me too!" Eddie confided with a snigger. "Tell me, if you were in my shoes, what would you do to resolve the issue and make the afternoon easier to train?"

"I'm not sure Eddie, I was thinking about that. Sometimes, one just needs to get negative thoughts off ones' chest, don't you think?"
"Yes, I do," he replied. "But in this instance, I think we can control her in that process. This afternoon, I intend to use my facilitation skills to help her get whatever is bothering her out into the open. At that stage, it's possible that her issues may be dealt with by the group, rather than me."

"I'm eager to see how you go about that, Eddie," Philip replied. "What about James? I sensed an increasing frustration from him that the session wasn't going fast enough to keep him interested."

"I agree," Eddie replied frankly. "And I have a plan for this afternoon. What I am going to do is catch James just before we restart after lunch and tell him: as he clearly has a good understanding of the topic, and how the change process works already, there are a few in the group that perhaps don't have his level of knowledge yet, and maybe I could call upon him from time to time, just to help me explain it to them? I am hoping that this will cause him to wait until I ask him to give his anecdotes and personal experiences rather than just butt in when I'm developing the concept for the rest of the group. What do you think?"

"Oh, I really don't know Eddie. I'm here to learn, but it sounds like it could work," Philip replied honestly.

Eddie continued, "I'm a little concerned about Esperanza though. She seems to have gone very quiet and is almost taking a back seat. I don't like to ask people questions directly…"

"Yes, I've noticed that!" Philip interrupted, pleased at last to have spotted something at the same time that Eddie had done. "Why *don't* you fire questions at people, Eddie? At least that will keep them on their toes and attentive to what is being taught."

"The way you phrased that is quite revealing, Phil," Eddie responded calmly yet firmly. "*Firing* questions at someone will only put them on edge and give them a sense of fear. They will be asking themselves 'what question will I get next? will I be able to answer it? etc' and I don't want people focussed on *that*, rather than on the message that they need to learn. Instead, you'll notice that when I ask a question that I want someone like Esperanza to answer, I will look at her, but don't use their name. I feel that this technique gives her the impression I am talking directly to her, but also allows her a 'way out' because I've not excluded the rest of the group. But the technique hasn't been working so far, if you've noticed, because James always chips in with the answer before anyone else has a chance to reply. Let's see if that changes after my chat with him?"

"That's an interesting plan, Eddie. I shall look out for that this afternoon," Philip stated. "There was another thing I was wondering about from this morning. Why do you ask so many questions? Wouldn't it be quicker to just tell the group?"

"Yes, it might be *quicker*," replied Eddie thoughtfully. "But what impact do you think it would have on their ability to recall the information after the training?"

"Oh I think I see what you mean. You are doing exactly the same thing to me now!" Philip mused. "You asked me a question so I had to work out the answer. It's as if you didn't need a response for your *own* knowledge, you just wanted me to think the problem through for myself."

"Exactly, Phil. María was right, you are quick to understand things and even quicker to apply them. The whole concept is that once they have made the mental connections in their own minds, they will be able to recall it quicker *and* be more committed to implement it," Eddie concluded, smiling warmly again.

"She said that?"

"Something like that, buddy. She likes you, I can tell."

"I'm sure she likes everyone," said Philip in an attempt to deflect the conversation away from anything too personal since he felt himself blushing and his breathing becoming shallower.

"I'm not so sure about that, Phil!"

FEEDBACK

When Philip returned to his chair at the back of the training room, waiting for the group to return, he sent María a text:

Hi María, how is your day? It's great to see some of the things that we've talked about, in action. I'm hoping you'll be able to give me some tips later on how to be as good a deliverer as Eddie is?x

After a few minutes, María's response buzzed through to his phone:

My day is going great, thanks for asking Phil. Glad to hear that you are getting loads from the day and, yes, I have some tips for you later!x

In haste before Eddie reopened the course, Philip wrote:

You are both awesome and lovely. Can't wait for this evening.xx

To which he received an almost immediate reply:

Nor me xx

Philip looked up from his messaging just in time to see Eddie finishing a conversation with James at the training room door. He smiled to himself knowing exactly what was being discussed between them. It looked to him as if James was in agreement with Eddie's suggested plan. Philip sat back, wondering what the afternoon would hold.

"That was a great day, I'm exhausted, but on such a high after it. Oh, and you look lovely!" the words escaped his mouth before he had the chance to check them. Philip immediately felt embarrassed at daring to offer a compliment at the start of the evening, but (he consoled himself) he was just being honest.

María was dressed in a black bodycon dress that was equally businesslike and feminine. Her long dark hair was flowing around her shoulders and her brown eyes twinkled at meeting Philip again.

"Thank you," she replied with a smile. "Tell me about your day?"

"It was really valuable María, but I am starving! Let's order food first and then I can fill you in on what I have learnt."

Once the food was ordered and the drinks served, Philip talked María through the day, including the conversations over the breaks with Eddie. He mentioned how Eddie had taken him through everything that he was doing and had helped him understand the mind of a professional trainer.

He concluded by stating: "There was one thing that I wondered about, which Eddie did. Before lunch, he gave me a copy of the slides he was covering in the session, but I couldn't work out why. I mean, it's not as though I was there to learn the content of the session, was it?"

"No, but let me ask *you* a question. Did you notice exactly how Eddie introduced each of the slides?" María asked.

"What do you mean?" he responded. "He pressed a button and the next slide came up on the screen!"

"Sure, but what immediately preceded him pressing the button? Did you notice that he almost always asks questions of the group, waits for their answer, and then the slide is brought up? What he invariably does is *reveal* the answer to his question by pressing the button and showing the slide. This technique of showing the correct answer via the medium of the slide, ensures that the group see a purpose in the visual aids."

"Oh he asked loads of questions throughout the whole day! I didn't realise that they were linked to the reveal of the slide until you just mentioned it, though. I guess he gave me the handouts so that I could work out what answer he was looking for from the group, before moving onto the next slide. All is clear now!" Philip said with the enthusiasm that comes when a taxing puzzle is finally solved.

"Yes, and the technique of asking questions is employed in order..."

"To ensure that the participants work things out for themselves rather than being spoon fed with all the answers!" interjected Philip, feeling like the star pupil with all the answers.

"Precisely right Padawan! But what I *was* going to say was that this technique is a part of the model I wanted to share with you tonight. This model is the result of research into the skills which top trainers use that make their training *memorable*. What it comes down to are several key elements." Whilst saying this, María reached into her bag and withdrew her note pad and pen. She started to list out the components on the pad:

• Procedure

- Ordering
- Informing
- Seeking
- Checking
- Supporting
- Demonstrating
- Summarising

"These are all the skills that a trainer could possibly use in the classroom, to a greater or lesser extent. In order to make their training a valuable experience they will need to balance the use of each correctly. Let me go through each of the skills and explain what I mean by each one."

As she individually defined the skills, María pointed to it with her index finger. Philip's gaze was caught by her dark nail polish that seemed to highlight the olive coloured skin of her long, slim index finger.

"**Procedure** is where you highlight what is going to happen in the session. It takes away the element of confusion and keeps people informed of your intentions and objectives of the session. It also prevents any potential disappointment later on.

"**Ordering** helps the learner to know exactly what they are supposed to be doing at any given point in time. Should they be taking notes? Asking questions? Or simply listening? Will there be handouts? Can they write on them? What should they do in the exercise? So, any aspect of the session which 'orders' the participants to *do* something.

"**Informing** is where the training provides information to the group. This can be factual or theoretical information. It's a statement that they make. You do not expect any interaction from the group during this, they are only expected to listen.

"**Seeking** is what you saw Eddie do a lot of today, by the sounds of things. This is the skill of asking questions to move the session along and build understanding of the topic. A trainer that is 'Seeking', expects an answer from the group or an individual.

"**Checking** is usually associated to 'Seeking' as this is where the trainer clarifies whether the participant *understands* what they have just said or learnt. It questions their breadth and depth of knowledge on the topic or exposes whether they are simply replying with 'hollow' words they don't understand. 'Checking' can be used by a trainer to dig deeper into the participants' answers to the previous questions.

"**Supporting** is so often overlooked. This skill is where the trainer verbally acknowledges the input of a particular participant. It's more than simply saying '*you're right*' as that is impersonal. 'Supporting' needs to be a very individual and personal statement. Instead, it should be '*You're right, Samantha*' or something like that. If the trainer's 'Support' isn't personal, it can come across as lacking sincerity and could be received negatively, turning the participants against the trainer.

"**Demonstrating** is a valuable skill, *sometimes*! It's the use of real life scenarios to illustrate the point being made. 'Demonstrating' isn't something that is always necessary as some sessions won't require it. The occasional use of anecdotes and stories of your experiences can help make the point 'real'. You don't want to go overboard with this though, because you don't want the training to degenerate into a session of telling stories or, worse still, all about the trainers' experiences!

"**Summarising** helps to gather all that has been said into bitesize and consumable pieces. It's the perfect finish to the session or topic as it consolidates all that has been trained in the session. This also doesn't want to be too lengthy, as otherwise it can confuse the group into thinking that this is new information that they need to note"

"All of this makes sense and I would say that at some point in their training, even the worst trainers I have encountered do all of these in a session," declared Philip.

"I'm sure they do," replied María. "But there is a 'perfect balance' between each of the skills that I am certain would separate out the 'good' from the 'bad' trainers."

"A perfect balance?"

Before she could respond, the waiters brought the food and they decided to eat and resume the conversation later. During dinner, María and Philip chatted about their hobbies, likes and dislikes and both avoided talk of work-related matters. Philip learned that María had come over from Spain when she was 18, had never gone to university, but was now studying for an organisational psychology degree in her spare time. She had a brother and a mother back in her homeland whom she visited on a regular basis and always felt homesick afterwards. Likewise, María discovered that Philip was an only child and had always found academia relatively easy. It was *people* that presented a challenge to him and this was why he had elected to go into sales. He had hoped being in sales would teach him how to 'read' people and understand them better, but admitted that he had gained success in sales without ever understanding why! She discovered his passion for ball sports and keeping himself physically fit and noticed an underlying competitive instinct in him.

"Where do you look upon as 'home' now?" Philip asked.

"That's a difficult question to answer. I suppose I look upon 'home' as where I'm *from* rather than where I am *now*, so I guess I would have to say Spain." After a moments hesitation, María continued. "But I suppose this is my home now. I don't know I will go back to Spain to live anytime soon."

"Why is that? Is there someone special here to keep you from returning?" Philip ventured with a cheeky smile.

"There hasn't been...but, maybe," she responded, returning the smile.

As the waiter collected their plates and provided them with the dessert menu, Philip couldn't help wonder whether María had a boyfriend in mind somewhere, or if her words were somehow directed at him. He realised that one answer filled him with a sense of dread. The other flooded his heart with elation; but before he was able to gain clarification from her on the point, she returned to the subject of the training skills.

"You asked what the 'balance' was between each of these skills or components. Obviously, it depends to a large degree on the topic or type of training being delivered; I mean, training someone to use a software package is, by necessity, going to demand the trainer use a lot of *Informing* and *Ordering* statements in their session. On the other hand, facilitating a group to come to a common consensus, will probably see a higher concentration of *Seeking* and *Checking* statements, rather than *Informing*. So, the researchers identified a band within which is found a strong balance."

"A 'band'? What do you mean?" he asked.

"It may seem a little scientific, but please bear with me on this. Imagine every comment, statement and question made by the trainer throughout the session as a whole, adds up to 100%. That percentage is then broken down into these component skills. Each time an *Informing* comment is made for example, a point is recorded against that skill, and at the end of the session, a percentage for each of the skills is calculated. So, every comment, statement or question that the trainer makes is recorded as a point which, in combination, add up to 100%; is this making sense so far?"

"I think so," replied Philip. "But I still don't understand what you are saying about the *balance* between each of these components?"

"OK. So, each component skill has a 'band' within which it was deemed to be an effective part of the session. A percentage return in excess of this band would indicate that the session became imbalanced, and therefore impacted the focus of the training. Any percentage below it would highlight that there was potential for confusion amongst the participants in the training, or that the session was information deficient somehow."

Sensing that Philip was still a little confused and was yet to grasp this principle, María continued.

"Let me work through an example for you," she said as she referred to her notepad at the page where she had written the eight components down.

"Imagine that the trainer was observed and in the session, the observer recorded these percentage scores for each of the components." María listed down the following:

COMPONENT	OBSERVATION
Procedure	6%
Ordering	1%
Informing	64%
Seeking	10%
Checking	2%
Supporting	0%
Demonstrating	12%
Summarising	5%

She spun the notepad round so it was facing Philip and asked: "What would you learn from this data?"

At first, Philip simply saw a mass of numbers that added up to 100%, but then, as he looked across each line and referenced it against his notes on the definition of the component skill, he began to get a picture of what the observer recorded.

"What I am seeing is that the trainer did a heck of a lot of *telling*, but not a great deal of *listening* to ensure that the group understood what was being trained."

"That's good so far Phil. Tell me why you say this?"

"The score for *Informing* is very high, more than half of the session appears to be the trainer talking *at* the group. On the other hand, there was hardly any *Checking* so I reckon the trainer wasn't really asking any questions to dig down into the group's knowledge and see whether they understood or not?"

"Great stuff Phil. So we need to know what 'good' looks like and by that I mean what scores are considered 'balanced'. The research concluded that within these bands, a session would *always* be effective, irrespective of the type of training being delivered."

Again, she wrote on her notepad:

COMPONENT	OBSERVATION	IDEAL
Procedure	6%	2.5-7.5%
Ordering	1%	2.5-10%
Informing	64%	13-28%
Seeking	10%	17-38%
Checking	2%	12-25%
Supporting	0%	8-15%
Demonstrating	12%	0-5%
Summarising	5%	5-10%

"Tell me, Phil, what do you notice about *these* figures?" María enquired.

After careful consideration, Philip responded by saying: "I'm not sure; there are a couple of things that I'm struggling to figure out, like how come *Informing* has a lower range than *Seeking*?"

"Uh ha. Anything else strike you as odd?"

"Yep, *Demonstrating* is the only component that apparently you can score 0% at and *still* be considered 'ideal'. Is that correct or an error?"

"No, that's quite right when you think about what *Demonstrating* actually is, Phil. Remember that it's defined as the anecdotes and references to episodes that have actually happened?"

Philip nodded a response, but sensed that this was a little fantastical.

"Well, if the training topic is on something that is brand new, totally original - it stands to reason that no anecdotes can exist to support the training. Hence a return of 0% would be entirely appropriate."

"I understand."

"You also thought that the bands for *Informing* and *Seeking* looked as though they should be reversed?" she continued. "It's funny, that's what everyone initially thinks, myself included. Perhaps it is something to do with our own experiences because we see so many trainers 'lecture' us, never appearing to want to involve us as participants in the session. No, the reality of the issue is that a *professional* trainer needs to get the brain cells of the participants stirring. Just like you saw today with Eddie. Questions stimulate responses in the brain, they create neurological pathways that can aid the learning process. Even if you don't answer my question when I ask it, your brain goes into action and starts to *try* to fathom out a response. That's the *real* role of a trainer, to get those thought processes in gear."

"But," Philip started unsure of where this conversation might take him. It appeared to him, that they were moving towards a slightly illogical conclusion. "But if *Informing* is such a low percentage, let's take it to the extreme and say it was at 13%, and *Seeking* was at the upper limit of nearly 40% of the session, wouldn't that mean that the trainer isn't doing their job?"

"Why do you say that?" María asked with a knowing smile.

"Because if the trainer is only *asking questions* and barely giving any information, surely that means that the participants are effectively training themselves?"

"Too right!" she exclaimed, the smirk still on her face. "What's the problem with that?"

"Well, that can't be good!" Philip snapped, slightly peeved. "I mean, surely that makes them an unprofessional trainer because they aren't adding any value to the session? Surely, any old fool could stand at the front of the classroom and fire a load of questions at the group and that would give them the 'ideal' score?"

He felt himself starting to lose belief in this system, and the research that it came from. Maybe María, as nice as she was, was now proving herself to be incompetent, out of her depth or guilty of 'over-thinking' this training delivery stuff?

"Sure, that could happen *if*, and only '*if*', the questions were asked in an 'unskilled' manner," María responded carefully. Again, as she spoke, she smiled knowingly. Philip's hackles were rising now as he believed these smirks indicated that she knew something he didn't, and was withholding information from him in order to watch him fail. This annoyed and frustrated him.

"Now I'm feeling a little lost, María. And what's with all your secret smiles after I say something to you? Do I have spinach in my teeth or what?" he shot at her.

He didn't want a response, he was feeling agitated, something about this scenario was annoying him. Maybe he was tired, maybe he was feeling the effect of the pressure to learn and remember all this information. Maybe he just wanted and easy life, a life where he could simply pitch into the training room and deliver his training without worrying about 'balancing component skills'. He knew he was getting tetchy and was unsure of his feelings regarding María. Was his brain feeling completely overloaded? or was he out of his depth with all this? After all, he considered, surely this wasn't necessary to remember in order to simply train someone?

"Sorry Phil." María said, her voice sounding grave and genuine. "I didn't mean for you to feel uncomfortable, it's just...."

"Just what? You are laughing at me because I'm such a novice? Because I know nothing?" Philip interjected sharply, anger rising. He was working himself up into a state of frustration and annoyance now and he knew it.

"I think we had better call it a night now. Thanks for your company this evening, but I really should be getting off home, " he said sharply.

"OK," María replied with a crestfallen look on her face. "Phil, I'm sorry if I offended you somehow. That was never my intention."

"Fine. I'll pay for the meal and get the restaurant to order us a couple of taxis," he said abruptly. It was clear to María that she had upset him and she needed to tread carefully now.

"I will pay half, it's ok."

"No, you won't. I invited you to dinner as a thank you for you help. OK?" It sounded more like a threat than a question, but María elected to let it lie.

"OK. Thank you," she said. "May I give you this card before we go? This is a great trainer that I worked with once on a huge government project, Nathan. He is an awesome coach and someone that really knows his stuff when it comes to training people. If you ever want someone to come and observe you, he is really good at giving some pointers, call him. He has an awesome reputation and an ever growing client list."

"Sure. Thanks," replied Philip in an off-hand manner that indicated he didn't think he would ever call this guy. However, he slipped the card into his jacket pocket and chalked this evening down to experience; never again mix business with pleasure, he told himself.

CHAPTER 11

HELP

"I really don't understand what happened, Gareth," declared Philip.

"It's just not good enough, Philip. We expected you to produce far better results than this. I mean, it's as if all of the people you have trained haven't understood a word you've told them. Were you speaking in a foreign language or something? You may as well have been, for all the effect it's had on these results!"

Gareth brooded over the latest quarterly results. Every measurement had gone down, except for the costs to profit ratio which had soared. The strategy that the board had spent a year constructing in order to move the company forwards, was now in jeopardy. Philip felt like he was being identified as the ideal scapegoat, a corporate patsy.

"I mean," Gareth continued. "Whatever you did with these people has clearly not worked, has it? You cannot let this happen. You need to rectify the situation immediately, or else I'm going to have to seek alternatives."

That last comment invited no further discussion. Both men knew exactly what it meant. Philip was looking down the barrel of the gun. He needed to do something radically different, or else he knew he would be fired. But what could he do differently?

Philip knew he may have completely disregarded all that psychological clap-trap about percentages, but he had followed María's *ABCD* format for session design. Each session, he reflected, felt as though it had gone well and the comments he received from several attendees was always positive. So how had he got it *so* wrong?

Over the next day or two, things took a turn for the worse. The results of the compliance test, that many of the staff were required to take, were returned. All of the employees had failed except for three. This was a pre-requisite for them to do their job. The three who passed were Philip's subject matter experts. If anyone should have passed, it should have been them! It was an indication that the training had failed. He had seconded the experts to deliver it, but (he reflected) had neglected to help them with their delivery skills. The result was clearly *not* 'memorable learning'.

As he sat at his desk, Philip felt at an all time low. How was he going to get himself out of the hole that he now found himself in? Failure was not an option, he determined. He *had* to find a way to get these results for the business.

As he contemplated his options, 'Maybe,' he thought, 'I should just bury my pride and call María for her advice'; but then thoughts of her smirking and laughing at him set his hackles up again and he elected not to go down that route.

Then it came to him. He had an option. If only he could remember what he had done with it. He rummaged around the drawers of his desk and eventually found it, creased and discarded at the very back of the drawer was the business card.

Nathan sat opposite Philip in the canteen. He was a slim, middle-aged man with a greying beard and grey hair, but he looked fit and healthy and had a friendly complexion that Philip immediately warmed to. As soon as he spoke, Philip realised he was not from this country and soon worked out he was originally from New Zealand.

"María said you might call me, but to be honest it's been a while since she said that and I'd forgotten all about you!" Nathan said lightly, to open the conversation.

"Yes, well..." Philip muttered, memories returning of the bad terms which lead to their parting at the restaurant sometime ago. He found his guilt over his tantrum that evening returning to him like a bad dream.

"So, tell me what has happened over the last month since you met her?" Nathan asked, sensing the awkwardness from the mention of María's name.

"OK. Well, I constructed the training sessions for the new web services we are now offering here. I used the *ABCD* structure that María taught me. But when I delivered the information, none of it seemed to hit the mark. In fact, I think I was wasting my time because no one that attended the training seems to have remembered a damn thing I said!" Philip was clearly agitated by these experiences; a fact that was not lost on Nathan.

"How do you know that your training had *no* impact?" Nathan asked passively.

"Last quarters' results were dire. Sales figures were down, solution sales were almost non-existent, service delivery response rates have also dropped. In fact, everything appears to have spiraled downwards following my training!"

"I see. And you are feeling under pressure now?"

"Yes I am," declared Philip with exasperation in his voice, but also sensing some relief at being able to share his plight with someone. "I am being held accountable for it, to a large degree, and my job is on the line as a result."

"Man, that's tough," Nathan empathised. "Another question: Did you train all the employees together, or how did you split up the training sessions?"

"I designed separate sessions for sales, support and back office staff."

"So, three sessions in total?"

"Well four actually. The first one was just in order to frame the changes that were happening within Woodroot Hosting. I then trained all the salespeople first, followed by the support staff and then I started working my way through all the administrative functions."

"And group size?"

"About 12 people per group."

"What about the managers?" Nathan explored.

"Yes I trained them at the same time as their teams," Philip stated.

"I see. Was there was any training specifically for managers?"

"No."

"Has all the training been completed, or do you still have some sessions to run?" Nathan asked, taking full notes of everything he was learning from Philip.

"I have the final session running tomorrow with the finance team, after that I'm done."

"OK, thanks for bringing me up to speed with where you are, Phil. I wonder whether I might sit in on the training tomorrow to get a feel for your style and content?"

"Sure, no problem," Philip replied, still wondering whether this was going to help him sort out his issues, or if he was simply wasting time and more company money. Quite frankly, he though, he had no choice anyway, this was the last roll of the dice.

CHAPTER 12

OWNERSHIP

"Thanks for letting me sit in on your session today, mate," Nathan said after the group had dissipated. "I've made a few notes throughout the day, do you want me to share my observations?"

"Yes, of course," Philip nervously agreed. 'Feedback' was always synonymous with pretty brutal criticism to him, usually leaving him feeling emotionally defeated and bruised. As a result, Philip felt himself immediately becoming defensive as Nathan spoke.

"OK, well first off, the room layout was great for the type of training you were doing. There was the ability to both talk to the group and see the eyes of every participant as you did so. Equally, they could discuss matters between themselves when the time called for it. I also liked the way that you greeted each person as they came into the training room, that made the whole session very personable and friendly and seemed to relax some of the less confident participants. Did you notice where the first people sat in the room?"

"Mmmm, let me see," Philip reflected, "Erica came in first, I think, and she sat directly opposite me. Then it was Uneeb who sat in the middle of one of the sides, didn't he?"

"Yes, and what did that suggest to you?" Nathan asked.

"Er, well, Uneeb said he had to sit there so he could hear everything."

"That may be true, but how much did he participate throughout the session?"

"He didn't."

"You're right. He remained very passive throughout the whole session. And what about Erica, what were her participation levels like, did you find?"

"Well, she was an 'active' member of the group! In fact there were times when her attitude kind of sucked!"

"Yeah mate, too right! She was a bit feisty wasn't she? I think that she came into the room with a bit of a chip on her shoulder! She seemed to have some views that she wanted to voice, or rather, offload! In what frame of mind do you think she left the training?" Nathan questioned.

"Pretty similar to how she came into the room, if I am honest Nathan," Philip stated, and then added. "But I don't have a problem with that."

"You don't?"

"No. Why should I? I have given her the information that she needs to do her job, it's not *my* problem if she refuses to use it," Philip declared in his defence.

"Isn't it?" retorted Nathan. It was as though he was batting a tennis ball back over the net to his partner, sparring with questions, verbal jousting.

"How can it be? I'm not her manager, nor am I responsible for her performance. If she is too arrogant to *use* the information I gave her, well, that's *her* problem, isn't it?"

"Maybe," Nathan stated carefully and after a slight pause. "But I thought you said that Gareth was looking to you to improve performance of the employees?"

"Yeah, he is," he replied sheepishly, knowing now where this conversation was leading.

"That makes it as much *your* responsibility as it does her manager, don't you think? And more than that, Phil, when she goes back to her desk is she likely to sit there in silence, or do you think that she might just continue her negative comments as she talks with her team?"

Philip reflected for a while, but didn't respond.

"If she talks to the team, slagging everything off, we stand the risk that she will influence her colleagues to disregard any of the changes you need," Nathan continued.

Philip took a few moments to think through what Nathan had said. He began to see the sense in it and where he may have made a serious error of judgement.

"So, what should I have done differently to prevent her walking out of the room negatively?"

"Only two things Phil."

Two? Philip thought. He had expected a whole list of changes and amendments he would be asked to remember and implement. Two was a relief and immediately he felt himself become more attentive and energetic.

"I want you to have a think about these two things," continued Nathan. "It's completely up to you if you want to use these ideas though Phil, or disregard them if you want, mate."

"Cool. What are they?" Philip asked with renewed vigour.

"The first thing is the order in which you trained people. I'm not talking about the order of the *departments* that you trained here mate; I'm talking about training the managers *and* their teams at the same time. Place yourself in the shoes of the manager for a minute. They came on the training at the same time as everyone else, but they will need to take in all of the information, convert it into a plan of how they will manage their team and then immediately dispatch the team to implement it. And this all has to happen within a few minutes of leaving the training room! Maybe we are not giving them a good enough chance to make the changes work? It's important as they are the people who are going to take your information, and make it happen out in the business. If there is one group that have the ability to make, or break, your training back in the workplace, it's the managers, Phil."

"What do you suggest? Separate manager sessions?"

"That's exactly what they need Phil. Their discussions need to be with other managers facing the exact same issues of implementing this new strategy with their teams. They need the information about the new services *before* their teams, *and* they need time to work out how they are going to manage the implementation of it."

"So, what I should have done is train the management population *before* anyone else, to give them time to work out how to put together their strategy for implementing it in their business area. I guess that if I had done that, the team might have hit the ground running after they left my training, or at least the manager might have immediately reinforced the learning at team meetings, one on ones etc?"

"You got it mate," declared Nathan enthusiastically.

"That makes a lot of sense. OK, what about the second thing?"

"Yeah, the second thing is more personal mate, it's about the way that you deliver your training."

The sinking feeling in Philip's stomach returned. He steeled himself for brutal criticism as Nathan continued: "I know that María took you through the eight component skills of a training session. She mentioned that there was a little skepticism about it? I understand why you feel that way, Phil, but I want to show you your scores."

"What do you mean *my* scores? Have you been scoring me all day?"

"I was mate. Whilst I was observing you, I was making notes on the type of comments and statements you were making. I think you may find something in this feedback that could significantly improve your ability and get the participants to buy into your message quicker. See what you think."

With these words, Nathan handed Philip the following chart:

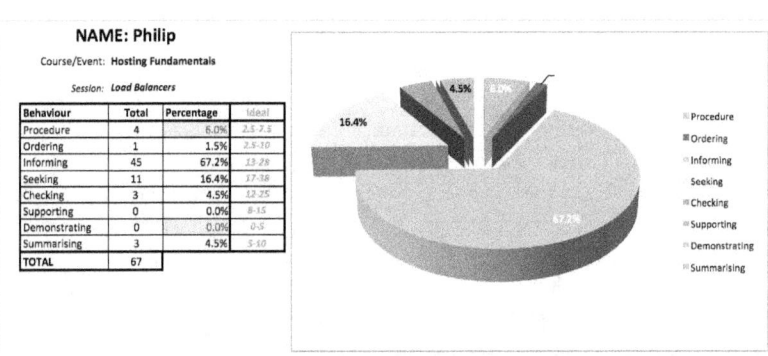

NAME: Philip

Course/Event: **Hosting Fundamentals**

Session: *Load Balancers*

Behaviour	Total	Percentage	Ideal
Procedure	4	6.0%	2.5-7.5
Ordering	1	1.5%	2.5-10
Informing	45	67.2%	13-28
Seeking	11	16.4%	17-38
Checking	3	4.5%	12-25
Supporting	0	0.0%	8-15
Demonstrating	0	0.0%	0-5
Summarising	3	4.5%	5-10
TOTAL	**67**		

Philip took it and studied it for a few minutes.

After a while, Nathan asked: "Well mate, what are your thoughts about that?"

"I'm amazed," Philip replied, astonished at what he had been presented with. "It felt as though I was asking a lot more questions than the score you recorded for *Seeking*. And the score for *Informing* is through the roof! I guess if I was looking at this chart as an observer that hadn't seen the session, I would say it was a lecture, not an interactive training session."

"That's a really cool observation, mate. You are working too hard!"

"What do you mean?" Philip enquired. Nathan now had his interest completely.

"I mean that you are doing *all* the work here. You are *telling* the group everything, rather than facilitating them to work it out for themselves. If you ask more questions than you do, what you'll find is that the participants will start to think things through in their heads for themselves. When they do that, you may find that they agree with what you are asking them to change more readily. Then they will simply keep quiet in the session and allow you to deal with those that don't get it; or they may chip in and support what you are saying, influencing the remaining group. If they don't get what you are saying, or they find they disagree, they will either ask questions or come out with negative comments, like Erica did today."

"And what do I do then? I mean I can see that it would be really easy for me to just answer any negative comments, but that will just add to my *Informing* score, won't it?" Philip asked.

Nathan was a man that enjoyed helping people and he now began to warm to Philip, recognising that here was a man that was really trying to do well, but was under pressure to achieve.

"You would, mate. If you answered her by giving further information or facts, even your opinion, it would add to that score. So what alternative solutions have you got?"

"I just don't know!" exclaimed Philip feeling the same as when a crossword answer is just on the tip of your tongue, but still out of reach.

"How would you have influenced someone to buy your product when you were out there selling?" Nathan asked using a slightly different tack that he hoped would put Philip back in his comfort zone.

"That's easy, I would ask them questions that would ultimately get them to say 'yes' to me!" responded Philip with a broad smile.

"And what's the difference here then?" asked Nathan, relieved that Philip had answered exactly as he had hoped.

"Oh..." Suddenly Philip had a moment of realisation. He now understood what María had been trying to get him to see when they had last met. He now appreciated that there was more than one way to train, that you could either tell them yourself, or you could nudge them in the right direction with questions, so that they could convince themselves. He now realised what an idiot he had been towards María. After all, she was only trying to help him, trying to get him to come to the exact same conclusions that Nathan had. And yet she was smirking at him all the time, making fun of him. Why would she do that? Philip felt a mixture of embarrassment and shame at his past behaviour and he resolved to try to rebuild the bridge that he had broken with María.

"Oh, you're good Nath!" Philip enthused. "You've done little more than ask me questions since we started, and you've simply got me to come up with all the answers myself, but I suspect they were the things you wanted me to say! That's brilliant!"

Philip was on a high, he felt as though he had finally seen the light and that light was well within his reach. He had a plan now. His plan was to simply 'sell' in the training room. He knew what he wanted the group to 'buy', all he had to do was treat it as a sale from the moment he walked into the training room. Something in his memory banks moved. Hadn't María stated that is what *she* did when she moved into training from sales? Eventually, his thoughts returned to Nathan.

"Totally mate, you've rumbled me. There is a saying that someone once said to me which goes *'If I say it, you can take it or leave it; but if you say it, you'll believe it'*. That's my mantra in the training room and I see our job as being the ones who help the group to come up with the 'right' answers, but without us having to tell them. So, *Seeking, Checking, Supporting* and even *Summarising* become the key components of any session we deliver. Think about what you want the group to think, say or do, and then phrase your questions in exactly the same way as you would do when you were selling."

"That makes so much sense. In fact, you have just reminded me of when I first met María. She said that she was told training was 'taking all her selling skills and simply moving them into the training room'. I get that now. Thanks Nath, I really appreciate it."

"No worries mate. Perhaps you can let me know when you are next training and I can see how your scores have improved?"

"That's a deal Nath. One last question: have you observed Eddie in María's team? That phrase you just used sounded familiar."

"Yeah, I did the same for him too, he's become a top trainer now though, no need for me anymore."

"Good to know Nath. And now I think I owe you a beer."

"Thought you'd never offer, mate. I'm gasping!"

CHAPTER 13

FOLLOWING UP

With renewed vigour over the next week, Philip worked hard on designing a training session exclusively for managers. He elected to provide an event to help them continue the transition to the new strategy, for both themselves *and* their teams. The content was focussed on helping the manager develop and coach their team to sell, deliver and administer the new product; Philip structured it using the now familiar *ABCD* framework that was becoming second nature to him now.

He and María had not spoken since the night he got upset with her for apparently laughing at him as he struggled to understand and appreciate the delivery skills framework. The more he thought about it, the more he felt ashamed and embarrassed at his behaviour, but he was reluctant to contact her again. He was struggling to pick up the phone and apologise to her too. He felt bad, not just for his own embarrassment, but because of the damage it had clearly inflicted on their relationship. María, he was now certain, had had his development at heart, but he still couldn't understand why she was laughing at him that night. It seemed so callous and unsupportive of him to smirk at his every thought or question. If only he could understand her, he thought. One thing was certain though, he needed help, but didn't feel he could call on her.

Instead, he called Nathan and arranged for him to come to observe his new session with the managers. Philip surprised himself as he prepared for the session; he found himself incredibly motivated to improve his scores in the components and deliver a 'professional standard' training course.

On the day of the training, he set up the room in the usual horseshoe shape, met up with Nathan and took him through his planned content for the course. He then greeted each participant as they arrived and chatted with them before the session started, using Eddie's technique to try to ensure he could recall their names when he needed to.

As he commenced the first session of the event, Philip opened with the words:

"Jack Welch, CEO of GEC, once said that 'Before you are a leader, success is all about growing *yourself*. When you become a leader, success is all about growing *oth-*

ers'. Today, we are going to work on developing an action plan to support the development of your team members and make them more successful than ever. Having been in the field myself until recently, I have a sound working knowledge of all of your jobs, but I've also spoken with your departments to get a feel for the pressures and difficulties you face with our new strategy. What we are going to do today is work through three things:

> • "Understanding the strategy in its entirety so you can articulate it clearly to your team,

> • "Design a training session that will support the implementation of the strategy in your business unit and,

> • "Identify your own action plan, including a coaching programme, that you can take back with you and start working with immediately.

"Now, does that work for everyone?"

When everyone indicated their approval, Philip continued. "Great. I have some handouts here that are designed to support your personal notes, so please jot down your own thoughts, or whatever you need to remember the things we discuss today."

Following this, Philip went through the agenda items, discussed breaks and outlined the expectations of the participants for the day, before inviting the group to introduce themselves. This he did by using the same method as he had seen Eddie do several weeks ago.

Throughout the day, Nathan noted that Philip made a particular effort to understand the problems that each manager believed they faced, and work with them to find the solutions. His excellent questioning skills, honed by years in sales, were in evidence as he invited the group to answer his questions; he then looked for clarification of their answers and eventually worked their responses into his training, ensuring that he gave them the credit. In fact, Nathan noted that each of the components were being ticked, even *Demonstrating* when Philip recounted a story of an experience he had in the field, to make his point.

A couple of times throughout the day, Nathan noted a few heated conversations between participants in the group. He carefully watched Philip to see how he responded and whether he dealt with the interruptions. On both occasions he watched as Philip effectively chaired the discussion, ensuring that both sides had sufficient opportunity to voice their opinions and concerns. He even encouraged the others in the group to give their thoughts, before bringing the conversation to a conclusion. Nathan sat back in his chair, impressed.

At the end of the day, the two men got together for a roundup on the events of the day. Nathan opened with his thoughts.

"Mate, can I just say from the start, you were awesome today! What an amazing improvement since the last time I saw you. I am so impressed. You've certainly absorbed everything that María has taught you. And you've clearly worked really hard to ensure it is all incorporated in your course. It's a tremendous success story."

"Thanks Nath. I appreciate that." Philip beamed a proud, yet troubled smile at the mention of María's name, memories returning. "What about my scores, how did they match up?"

"See for yourself," said Nathan as he slipped Philip his scores on a sheet of paper.

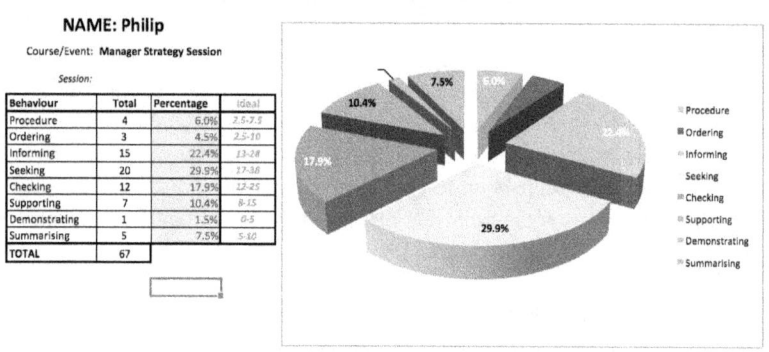

NAME: Philip

Course/Event: **Manager Strategy Session**

Session:

Behaviour	Total	Percentage	Ideal
Procedure	4	6.0%	2.5-7.5
Ordering	3	4.5%	2.5-10
Informing	15	22.4%	13-28
Seeking	20	29.9%	17-38
Checking	12	17.9%	12-25
Supporting	7	10.4%	8-15
Demonstrating	1	1.5%	0-5
Summarising	5	7.5%	5-10
TOTAL	**67**		

"It really couldn't get much better, mate. I'm so proud of you and I'd bet María would be too," Nathan stated with an equally huge smile on his face that supported his praise. "Tell me, how did that session feel, in comparison to the last one you did?"

"It was much more fun. I would even say it was a lot easier because I did't feel I had to make all the statements. Allowing the group to make my points for me is certainly a lot more enjoyable than making them all myself. All I had to do was 'load the gun for them to fire'!"

"It certainly felt that way from my perspective, too. Mate, the whole atmosphere seemed so much more relaxed. I no longer had the feeling that I was sitting in a 'classroom' listening to 'teacher'. It felt like you were working *with* the group in order to achieve something really good and valuable for everyone."

The praise made Philip feel a little giddy through a mixture of relief and joy. Until he was brought back to reality with a jolt in Nathan's next question.

"Now, buddy, what do you have planned for the next steps?"

Confusion flooded his brain. Next steps? He had just finished the training, this was surely the conclusion, the end, the completion of his work?

"Next steps?" Philip repeated quizzically.

"Yeah mate. What are you going to do next to ensure that, what the managers have learnt and agreed to action, is actually implemented back in the workplace?"

"Er....I, er..," stammered Philip feeling as though this question had caught him off guard like a heavyweight boxer landing a sucker punch on his opponent. "I...er...haven't really thought about 'following up' at all, Nath. Is that something you would normally do?"

"Certainly mate. In fact, it's the next level in your pyramid that María is working on with you. Did she talk with you about the 70-20-10 principle?"

Philip nodded his response.

"She probably mentioned that about 20% of all learning is said to take place outside of this training room, through what we term *Facilitative Learning*?"

Again, Philip nodded, then asked: "Remind me what that means again?"

"You know, things like on-the job training, coaching, manager support that sort of stuff? Well, how are you supporting *that* learning? Or do you have some mechanism to just make sure it actually happens out there?"

"Er...I don't know! Like I say, I was just focussed on getting through the training course!"

"I understand buddy. Failure to follow up your training, though, is another of the reasons why trainers *disengage* with the business. If *you* don't follow the learning through to the very end, it becomes too easy for the training skeptics to claim it was *they* who achieved the good business results, not your training."

"Oh, well...er...yes, I suppose I did the same when I was in the field. Any suggestions what I should do, Nath?" Philip felt like a schoolboy that had just realised he had forgotten to do his homework and had come clean to the teacher.

"Yes mate. I think you should book the same managers into another session in, say, six weeks from now to discuss their findings, results etc. It doesn't have to be a long event like today, but there needs to be a 'stake in the ground' or a point in time by which they need to have implemented their action plans."

"OK, I can do that," Philip stated, a mixture of relief and renewed enthusiasm. "Shall I set them the task of preparing a short presentation for that event. That way they can share what they have done, learnt and the impact it has had on their business unit or team?"

"Sounds like a great plan to me Phil," replied Nathan.

"Nath, you mentioned that this was the next piece in the pyramid that María was sharing with me, but what is that piece actually called?"

Nathan went to one of the whiteboards in the room and drew the pyramid from the bottom upwards. "You have already looked at three of the five *disengaging influences* that trainers do wrong: their lack of proper research, ineffective design of the training and inappropriate delivery. Is that right?"

"Spot on."

"Good. This level, then, is simply what we have discussed today. It's a huge pitfall that many trainers *assume* will happen outside of the training room, but they seldom check or enforce it. In fact, I would go so far as to say I don't often see trainers even encouraging it to happen. It's *The Failure to Follow Up* on the training."

As he said this, Nathan drew the next level of the pyramid diagram:

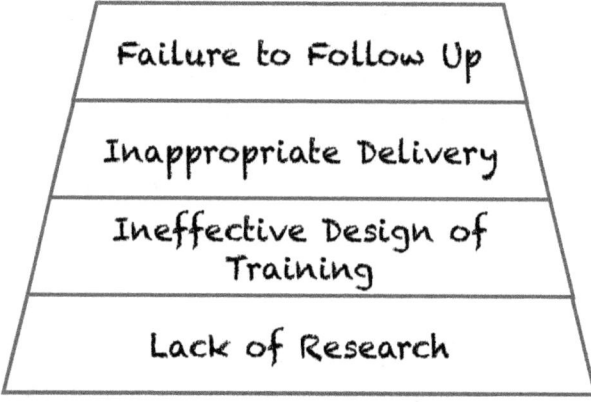

"I'm certainly guilty as charged on that count!" joked Philip. "But how on earth am I ever going to get to follow up on each of the people I have trained? There's likely to be hundreds by the time I've finished. I can't possibly get around to that many people!" he fretted.

"Don't worry. There's no need, my friend," Nathan calmly stated. "What we have just been discussing here, you know, this follow up for the managers is a form of it. It could take the form of a second training event, but it could equally be that you go and observe participants, just as I have done with you today, in fact!"

Philip thought back to his previous conversation with Nathan, when he had observed his first training session. He recalled now that Nathan had suggested coming back to observe him again and assess his improvement. It seemed, at the time, a perfectly logical and viable plan.

Nathan continued. "Additionally, it could be that you just chat with the individuals or view them out in the field, or you could even take the time to coach them individually perhaps? Some trainers send out follow-up questionnaires to ask what they have done differently after the training. This is useful for large scale follow ups."

Philip thought of the possibilities and what might be the most appropriate for his training events. Nathan continued: "There are a number of ways that it can be followed up, just be creative. Oh, and remember one thing," he added as an afterthought like the tv character Detective Columbo was famous for. "It doesn't have to be *you* that follows up the training. It can be their line manager or even an independent person. Just knowing that the training doesn't end the minute they walk out of the training room, is enough to keep the message front of mind for most participants and make certain something changes."

"That sounds like a great idea. I'll put some thought into that and see what I can come up with for the training that I have already delivered."

"Cool. Well mate, I need to dash. I wish you all the very best with what you do in the future. I'm always at the end of the phone if you need me, but then again I expect you'll be calling María if you need help. She has every confidence in you mate," Nathan stated with a glint in his eye and a wide smile on his face.

Philip's heart dropped at the mention of her name again; he couldn't get away from his predicament with María. He knew he was being pigheaded, stubborn and even denying himself the chance to learn from her, but he couldn't help it.

As he sat alone in the training room looking at the scoresheet Nathan had left him, he felt elated by the clear improvements shown in Nathan's observation. Yet he also felt as though something was missing. As he questioned himself on exactly what it was he felt was missing, he came to the a sudden realisation. He concluded that, despite receiving some great news today, news that he wanted to shout about to his nearest and dearest, it just didn't feel as good as it should. He realised what it was that he was missing, and also what he needed to do to remedy the problem. In his moment of triumph, Philip realised he missed her company more than ever.

CHAPTER 14

AWARDS

"Er...hi...er...hola?" Philip stammered as he gripped the phone a little too tightly and pressed it hard against his ear. It had taken all his will power to overcome his embarrassment, and fear of rejection, and call her.

"It's Phil here. I...er...just wanted to say that I'm...er...sorry for not calling before and...er...well, I'm sorry for...well...being such an idiot, an utter buffoon."

He awaited her response. He waited to learn his fate. Had he blown their friendship? Had he blown the chance of more than just a friendship perhaps? In fact, maybe she didn't even want to know him anymore. Maybe she had found someone else? Was she happily in the early stages of a beautiful relationship with another? Maybe he shouldn't have called her?

He waited for a response. Any response. He waited for what seemed like hours. In fact it was no longer than a couple of seconds. Eventually, María's voice came through his handset.

"But why you are a baboon? I no understand."

Not only was the silence broken, but also the ice. Philip smiled and replied.

"No, not a 'baboon'! I said a 'buffoon'. It means to be an idiot, a clown."

"Oh, I see. You have a big red nose now, like a clown? Why are you telling me this?"

The conversation was not going as Philip had rehearsed it in his head. Why did he use stupid English sayings when simplicity was called for?

"No...I..."

"I'm just teasing you Phil! It's good to hear your voice."

"Oh!" he sighed with relief. "I'm so sorry for the way I spoke to you at dinner, María. You didn't deserve that."

"It's fine, Phil," María started slowly, carefully selecting her words. "I have to apologise to you too. You said that I was laughing at you..."

"Yeah, I know I said that. I was such a fool. I am so sorry," he cut across her.

"No! I wanted to explain *why* I was smiling at you. I want you to know what I was thinking that caused me to smile like that. You see, the things you were saying were almost identical to the things that I said, when I was first shown the delivery skills framework. You see, cariño, I had a similar conversation with my mentor, Sylvia. I was initially just as skeptical as you were. I had misgivings and expressed them in the same manner as you. I completely understood where you were coming from when you said those things."

If anything, these words were making Phil feel even more wretched. If only he had allowed her to explain herself at the time, rather than rushing out the building at the speed of sound, he thought.

"Thank you for being open with me about that María. In fact, I have come to the realisation that you were right all along about what you were trying to say to me. You've been really patient with me, and all I've done is throw it back in your face. I'm so sorry."

Philip's words cascaded from his lips but were originated from his heart, and María didn't need to use her empathetic abilities to hear how genuine he was.

"I also wanted to say," Philip continued, knowing that he was on a roll now. He felt he needed to say everything that was on his mind before he lost his courage. "I have missed your company. You have become one of my best friends and, well, I've missed our friendship these last few weeks."

"I have too, Phil. I enjoy your company and I love to talk with you about training too. Somehow it has made me reconsider why I do what I do, and reflect on whether I am practising what I preach. I've changed a couple of things in our training set up here as a result, and I reckon it's improved the quality of our training."

"That's great!" said Philip realising that he was, in reality, relieved that their discussions were not only for his benefit.

"In fact, we have been nominated for an industry training award and I think it is down to some of these changes we have made, after discussing things with you."

"Now *that* is really very impressive, María, congratulations!"

"Thanks. It would be lovely if you would come to the awards dinner.....as my guest? But I would understand if you didn't want to."

Philip initially assumed that the last part of her comment was a question, but was a little reluctant to make a fool of himself for a second time. So, in the end he merely asked about the occasion, date and dress code. Using his well-practised questioning skills, he eventually ascertained that she would be going with members of her team, each of whom was able to bring a partner. With an increasing sense of excitement, Philip realised she was actually asking *him* to go as her 'date'.

"So, will you come with me?"

As she asked, Philip felt his heart summersault; his mouth dried up and words rushed in and out of his head, none seeming to spring forth from his lips. Finally, he croaked his response: "That would be nice."

Nice? *Nice?* he thought. What sort of imbecile uses the term '*nice*' in reference to a date? He chastised himself and berated his low-level response that must have given her the impression that he was not at all keen. Not for the first time, embarrassment filled him at his lack of coolness around her.

Over the next few days, Philip was on a massive high. His world seemed to be becoming a much more comfortable and colourful place. Not only were the managers now seeking him out to discuss their training plans with him for their team, but also some had asked him to sit in on *their* training and coaching sessions. This was so that he might give them feedback on their performance and improve the quality of their conversations. But more than that, much more than that, Philip had the awards dinner to look forward to, with María.

The awards were to take place in a swanky hotel in the city. As expected for such a prestigious event, it was a black tie affair. Philip always enjoyed putting on his black dinner jacket and bow tie, he was once told he looked like Daniel Craig's James Bond, which made him feel great. Somehow any evening was made more special as a result of wearing this outfit and this evening was no exception.

They had agreed to meet at María's apartment and catch a cab from her house, so when she greeted him at the door and invited him inside, Philip was aware that this was the first time they had met on anything other than 'neutral' ground. As María put the final touches to her outfit in her bedroom, Philip looked around at the room he had been directed into.

It was a tidy, if small, apartment with modern furniture. The walls were either stark white, or a terracotta colour which he put down to her Spanish nationality. He looked at the pictures on the walls, some were modern art in wild and dazzling shapes and colours that meant nothing to Philip. Others were photographs of María with, what he assumed to be, various family members.

"Well, what do you think? Do I look ok?" María asked nervously, when she finally emerged from her room. She was wearing a long, red dress that hugged her curves and showed off her figure perfectly. Her heels added a few extra inches to her height and placed her so she was almost as tall as Philip. She wore her hair down, but had curled it into black ringlets that seemed to enhance the beauty of her face and bring out the colour of her brown eyes.

Philip just stood there. He couldn't move. He certainly couldn't speak; his tongue was now glued to the roof of his mouth and was never going to cooperate with words. He was staring at her in what could only be described as a stupor.

"Is it too much? Should I change?" she asked, clearly taking his silence as a negative sign. She turned to retreat back to her bedroom.

"NO!" Philip almost shouted in a fit of fear. He surprised himself, startled himself even, but he could say nothing more. His eyes were still fixed on the thing of beauty before him, he was not able to break his gaze.

"O-K...," María said slowly, turning to face him whilst trying to work out what had happened to Philip. "Should we go down to the taxi then? I believe it is waiting for us."

"Er....y...yes, I suppose we should," Philip replied as if on autopilot and still unable to take his eyes of her. "Er....you look *amazing*, María!"

"Thank you," giggled María. Now it was clear that she had succeeded in making Philip completely dumb, as a result of her outfit. "You don't scrub up so badly yourself, Mr Bond!"

When they arrived at the dinner, María introduced Philip to the other guests at her table. He was grateful for recognising one face around the group, Eddie. The remainder consisted of members of María's team and a few individuals from around the business. Everyone had dressed in their most stunning outfits, including the men. One of them, Pratik, was even wearing a white jacket as a nod to Roger Moore's depiction of Bond.

"It is Pratik's work that has got us nominated for this award," María explained to Philip as she introduced him. "Pratik runs the on-boarding programme for the whole company and he has recently revamped it, based upon some of our conversations."

The wine flowed, the food came to the table, and empty plates were taken away. Pratik, who was clearly the central figure for this evening, readily told anyone and everyone who would listen what they had done for their submission. He went on to explain how he had implemented several changes over the last few months, following discussions with his boss, María. Philip listened with interest, trying to identify the links between the changes made, and his discussions with María. Throughout the meal though, María and Philip were never far from a conversation. They talked about work first; Philip brought her up to speed on what had happened over the previous weeks and how Nathan had helped him make significant improvements to his delivery style. María explained what was happening in her organisation regarding their acquisition and the potential impact on her. Then the conversation opened up and strayed to cover anything and everything. Once again, Philip was struck with the ease and comfort with which he talked to her. When they spoke, it was as though the world around them didn't exist and this was such a time. Their conversations were ultimately brought to a halt, though, by the MC stating loudly over the pa system: the awards were to be announced.

GOOD NIGHT

"Thanks for an amazing evening, María. I have so much more to learn from you and, who knows, one day I may well get an award of my own to bring home!" Philip chirped.

The evening had been a success on several fronts. Firstly, María's team had won the category for the best *Induction Programme* thanks largely to a stunning video sent in submission for the award. Pratik was ecstatic, and clearly celebrated harder than the rest of the team as a result, his moment of fame. It had been a fun evening for Philip too. He had found himself incredibly proud of María when she took to the stage with the team and accepted the award. Her words of acceptance were, of course, fo-cussed on the effort and devotion of Pratik. Although she took no credit for his suc-cess, she did mention the conversation with Philip that led to the changes that had the impact. During that part of the speech, Philip found his heart skip a beat and a tidal wave of emotion overcame him. He could not decide whether these feelings were the result of María's words, though, or the champagne that they had been drinking throughout the meal. He was certain of one thing-he felt the full strength of the con-nection between himself and María. He realised that she was a very special person, and that he enjoyed her company more than any other person he had spent time with throughout his working life. But he also knew she was no longer simply his business mentor.

"I meant everything I said about you in my acceptance speech, Phil," she said. "Had you not have asked me the questions that you did; or had we not have had our mentoring sessions, I doubt that I would have ever thought to challenge the way Pratik had designed and delivered his training. Part of this award is down to our friendship, and how highly I think of you."

Philip felt that he was not worthy of this praise but, nevertheless, he realised it was heartfelt and genuine. To object to it, could be seen as both ungrateful and even insulting, so in response he said:

"Thanks María. I think the world of you too."

The last statement spilled out of his mouth before he could even grasp his thoughts. He hadn't meant to be so personal and now he felt his face begin to colour in utter, mortified embarrassment.

"That's a lovely thing to say, Phil. You are a lovely man and I'm so pleased that we have become so close. I hope we will be friends for a long, long time."

The words were, once again, heart-felt, but this time Philip felt his spirits deflate as fast a balloon let go by the inhaler. He found himself focussing on the word 'friend' which María used to describe their relationship. He felt his heart being crushed like an empty coke can under a foot. He hoped they might be more than mere friends. Had he misread her feelings toward him *again*? Was he about to make a fool of himself once more?

They took a cab to the train station where they were to part.

"Well, thanks again for inviting me this evening, María," Philip said with as light a heart as he could manage with a shattered heart.

"There is no one I would have rather shared this evening with, than you, cariño," replied María, her brown eyes looking deeply into his pools of blue. After what seemed like an eternity without words, Philip instinctively leant towards María. Naturally, María moved her head a fraction towards him. Their lips brushed against each others, lightly at first before pressing harder into their new found partner. Philip's hands gently caressed María's face. María wrapped her arms around Philip's shoulders as their passionate embrace flowed over with months of emotion spilling out into the night sky.

There was no doubt about it, Philip mused as he sat on his homebound train a while later, this had been a 'great' night.

CHAPTER 15

RESISTANCE

"You want to do WHAT? Take my managers out of their workplace for *another* training session?" Gareth's annoyance was clear for Philip to see. "But I thought you had already trained them on the new products? Are you telling me you did *such* a bad job at it, that you need a second bite at the cherry?"

Philip knew that he had exhausted Gareth's patience.

"No, Gareth, I'm not saying that at all." Philip spoke calmly, attempting to defend himself.

"Then what are you saying? only, I'm having trouble equating why you keep taking people off the floor in order to sit them in your cosy little training room for days on end."

Gareth was an imposing man of Irish descent. He was well known for being a hard-liner, someone that did not suffer fools gladly. Actually, he didn't suffer them at all. In fact, he had a reputation amongst the employees in the company for being quick to judge people, and slow to change his mind. He was never going to be anyone's 'best friend', he did not have that persona. He would crack the occasional joke with people when he was in a good mood, but everyone was well aware that a bad one was never too far away. This caused his direct reports to always be on edge when he was around, to take care with the words that they used in front of him. They had all been on the end of his cutting comments and persistent (if uncomfortable) analysis of their intent behind the words they used.

Gareth was a man who was used to getting his own way. A man who seemed to know what he wanted and almost always ensured that he had the last word. He did not encourage people to think for themselves, or to question his decisions. Philip had fallen foul of him several times before, usually when he had found himself speaking out in direct opposition to Gareth's viewpoint. It had almost always ended with a metaphorical slap in the face.

"I have been in this business for decades," he continued. "And I can tell you that training is *not* about sitting around having nice cosy chats with people."

"No?" replied Philip, still attempting to remain calm and rational. "Tell me, what is training about exactly?"

"Quite frankly, I'm surprised and disappointed I have to spell this out to you. After all, we have invested a lot of time and money into getting you up to speed with the whole business of training."

"Please, indulge me. I would welcome your view on this. What do you understand 'training' to be?"

"It's simple. You are making it far too complicated, muddying the waters with all this psychological crap. Training is simply about taking people into a room, educating them on what they have to know or do better, and then shipping them out of the room...and the quicker you get them through that process, the quicker they get out there and do their proper jobs."

"So, just so I fully understand what you're saying, you believe it's about the trainer *telling* the staff what to do. Nothing more, nothing less?"

"At last! The boy get's it!" Gareth exclaimed, sarcastically.

"Ok," Philip appeared to consider for a moment. "If that's the case, then how can we be sure that the trainees actually put the training into practice out in the workplaces?"

"This is like teaching a five-year-old," Gareth muttered under his breath. "Because *that* is the job of their manager. The manager needs to ensure that the stuff you teach is put into practice in the real world!"

"I understand," responded Philip, giving the impression that he was in agreement. Just as he turned to walk away, though, Philip asked: "But how do we know the *managers* both understand and are making it happen in their teams?"

"Clearly," stated Gareth with an air of exasperation and a tone that he might use with a petulant child. "Clearly if the management are not making it work in their teams, it will show in their monthly performance figures."

"Yes, I get that. And if their figures are poor? What do we do with the managers or teams then?"

"Have you lost all memory of the last decade, Philip? I cannot believe we are having this mundane conversation! If you don't perform, you are disciplined, placed on a 'Performance Improvement Plan' or even fired! You *know* all this, why are you even asking me these pathetic questions?"

Evidently, thought Philip, Gareth's gaelic temper was beginning to flare up in Philip's face once again. He steeled himself to remain firm and continue his line of reasoning.

"Because, if the individual is placed on an 'Improvement Plan' one of the expectations is that they will, amongst other things, receive all the *training* that they need, in order to achieve success, right?"

Without waiting for a response from Gareth, Philip continued.

"And if the training is exactly the same as it was the first time around, which obviously didn't produce the right results, then what hope have we got of ensuring that the individual can turn things around?"

"So then we fire them; but at least we can do that with a clear conscience that we have tried our best and done all we can to help them change," Gareth stated in his usual emphatic and confident manner.

"Then *this* is where we fundamentally disagree, Gareth. I believe we have neglected to do our best and have failed to give the individual a fair crack of the whip."

These words came a surprise to Gareth, who up until this point had firmly believed that he had put a watertight and clear message forward, and no one on earth could argue against.

"What language are you talking now? Are you mad?"

"No Gareth. Look, if you sent me to a lecture on the intricate workings of brain functionality, disease and repair methods I would have *learnt* a lot, but there is no way I could ever go into the operating theatre and practice brain surgery, is there? You tell me to read a whole host of text books, discipline me all you like, but I just could not perform what I was expected to perform. Are we at least agreed on *that* point?"

Gareth nodded.

"So, you might want me to go to a few more lectures perhaps, or observe a few operations before you let me loose on a real patient?" Philip added.

"Sure."

"And even when you gave me the scalpel for the very first time, I'd guarantee that you'd be right there looking over my shoulder, telling me what to do and making certain I didn't kill the patient with my first incision, wouldn't you?"

"Probably, but what has this got to do with training for Woodroot?" Gareth asked, a little calmer than he was before.

"It's the same with our people. We can't just take them through the training room, like a flock of sheep passing through a sheep dip, and expect them to miraculously know and understand *everything* that was learnt in the room. And then apply all that information perfectly in the outside world, first time out. When we were at school, we sometimes had to learn things by rote. To do that, we might have employed many *different* methods: repetition of the times table perhaps, singing of nursery rhymes maybe? All of these learning methods demanded us to repeat and learn from experience. We have to *try* it for ourselves, often failing before we truly *learnt* how to do it on a consistent basis."

"Get to the point Philip!" Gareth cut in sharply.

"The point is that in order to *save* time and money, I need to be allowed to do a 'proper' job by training them. And in order to do that, I need to establish some form of repetition, some way of ensuring that the people I train are correctly performing what they've learnt, out in the field. I need to know they are doing it *right*. It may sound like I am spending a lot of time training people *now*, but if I can get them to do it right immediately, there will be no need for any remedial training or performance plans *later*."

"So you want to take them off the floor now in order to fix any bad habits that are being formed, before things get out of hand?"

"Exactly," stated Philip emphatically.

"Ok. Make it happen," Gareth stated as he turned to walk away, fortuitously, as Philip could not help but allow a victorious smile to spread across his face.

CHAPTER 16

COMMUNICATION

Over the next few weeks, Philip was busy working directly with the managers across all of the business units. Catherine, known simply as 'Cat', and Philip had joined Woodroot at the same time, going through the induction process together and learning how the company worked.

"I'm hearing good things about what you are doing for the company, now, Philip," she told him. "It seems as though your coaching is getting through to the teams and there is significant improvements as a result."

"Yes, I heard that the corporate results for the quarter have shown a good upward trend. I'm not sure that I can take credit for it though!"

"Oh, I don't know about that Philip. We all had the opportunity to make that change and sell solutions instead of products. All of the managers had their chance to make it work, but we couldn't make it happen alone. We just didn't have the time to work out *how* to make it work or *what* we needed the teams to learn. We didn't think about what we wanted to see change, or how we were going to coach the individuals *to* change. But then you came along and just gave us all the answers! and that really helped us because we just didn't have the time to think about it for ourselves," Cat explained.

"Thanks," replied Philip a little sheepishly. "But what have you done to implement the changes?"

"For a start, I set my team up for the training the way that you suggested in your session with the managers. I took some time in one of our team meetings to advise them of what was coming, why it was coming, and what were my expectations following their training. I even went to the extent, as you suggested, of telling them what *my* role would be, you know, to support and coach them through the changes."

"That's great, Cat. How did the team react?"

"At first, they were all moans and groans complaining that the company was implementing yet *another* change. I allowed them to offload all their negativity as I felt it was necessary to let them get it off their chests. As it happens, this was the best policy as all their dissatisfactions, arguments and disagreements with the changes were put on the table. Some were clearly angry, others worried."

"It's good that they opened up to you, Cat. How did you feel at this stage of the proceedings?" Philip asked.

"To be honest, I was struggling to deal with so much negativity. I mean, there didn't seem to be many of the team that could see any value or even hope for these changes."

"So, what did you do?"

"After they had opened up as a team, it was expected that I would respond with some corporate line, or agree with them. I didn't want to join their negative club, but nor did I want to come across as unauthentic. So, I elected to talk them through the impact on the future of the company if we continued as we have done in the past with the *same* products and the *same* results. I think that most people acknowledged that if we continued doing the same things, then everything would just degenerate into a price war, and Woodroot is never going to win *that* battle. So at least we all agreed that, on that basis alone, something had to change."

"Sounds good so far. What happened after that?"

"I then outlined about three possible alternatives that the organisation might have chosen, highlighting the issues associated with each. By involving the group in this process, we found that the best option was, in fact, the one that the company had chosen."

"That's great Cat. And the end result of this discussion?"

"Well, after a few of these conversations, I created tasks to implement the changes with the team. These tasks I shared amongst the members of my team and gave them full autonomy over *how* they would achieve them; all I asked of them was an update on progress, at each team meeting."

"Good plan! How has the task completion gone since then?" Philip asked, keen to know what was happening at the team level.

"That is what we are going to find out this morning at our team meeting, Phil. I'm hoping you have the time to come and observe the group and give me your thoughts on how enthusiastic, or otherwise, they are?"

"Of course, I'd love to come and see."

Philip sat at the back of the meeting room and subconsciously made an observation that the room layout was in the shape of a boardroom table. He smiled as he caught himself thinking that such observations had become send nature to him now.

Cat had placed herself at the head of the table in the role of chairperson. As the group filtered in, some were laughing and joking (Philip noted their positivity), but others were more subdued and quiet, taking their seats in silence and avoiding eye contact with Cat.

She opened the meeting with a few housekeeping issues, then she announced the team successes and stats from the previous period, before moving the meeting to the tasks she had set her team a couple of weeks earlier.

"Richie, you were asked to put some thoughts together over how we can best set up the sale from a skills perspective. Would you tell us where you are with that?" Cat asked.

"Sure," Richie responded. He was a dark-haired handsome man that, Philip speculated, spent half his life in the gym pushing weights. "I worked with both Kerry and Aman on this. We spent a little time discussing what the differences in skills might be needed between selling a 'product' and selling a 'solution'. We also researched some sites on the web. The result was that we basically felt that selling a solution was going to involve a heck of a lot more questions than we have been used to asking."

'Yes!' Philip thought. 'I *knew* that would be the case and tried to show everyone with the first training I did! Shame I went about it all wrong, but at least I know to trust my gut feeling.'

"More than that," Richie continued. "We felt that asking the questions to sell a product is easier because you know *exactly* which feature is going to sell to the customer; whereas with a solution, we are going to be in the dark most of the time we ask questions! So, we reckon we need a framework for asking questions that acts like a funnel, starting broad and then tapering down to something that we can sell. I suppose in the tapering, we need to expose customer problems and issues, but not to answer them until we have *all* the information and can design a full solution."

Philip felt smug.

"Sounds great Richie. Good job. Tell me, what do you anticipate the result of this approach to be, *if* we manage to get this framework organised?"

"We anticipated that, rather than selling *one* product to a customer, we are more likely to sell *multiple* products to them."

"Awesome; when will you be able to present us with a proposal for that questioning funnel you mentioned?"

"Already started work on it, Cat. It should be ready to discuss next meeting, but, Phil, perhaps we could ask *you* to get involved in this too? I think you have some good material you shared with us a while back?"

"Absolutely, Richie. I'd love to be involved."

"Great work Richie. Thanks Kerry and Aman for supporting with this. Let's table the new framework for next meeting," Cat continued. "OK, next on the agenda I have Emma who was working on the marketing process for solutions rather than products. How has that been going Em?"

As the meeting unfolded, one thing that struck Philip was how the team were clearly working together as a unit, for the common good. Cat was obviously their accepted leader, but she was inclusive of her team when decisions needed to be made. This style was noticeably working and her team were unified in their drive to achieve success. Philip also noticed, however, that Cat allowed the quieter members of her team to remain silent throughout the meeting. Two of the team were happy to sit in the shadows and would only speak when spoken to by Cat, otherwise they were nothing more than non-participative individuals in the team.

"So what did you think?" asked Cat after the group had left the room.

"Thanks for the chance to sit in today, Cat. OK, my observations are these. I felt as though you and your team are a pretty cohesive unit that seem to be working together in the same direction. I loved the fact that there is shared responsibilities *and* that you are holding them accountable for their actions. Most of them seem to be positive about the changes and the direction that the team is heading," Philip explained.

"Hold on," Cat cut in. "You said *most* of them?"

"Yes, I did Cat. This is one of my suggestions for you to look at in the future. Did you happen to notice the involvement levels in the meeting of the two that were sat in the corners of the room: Aurelie and Jordan?"

"Not really, no. I couldn't really see them most of the time because they were sitting behind Deanna and Mario." Cat replied a little on the defensive.

"They were, I guess. Maybe they selected those places with the intention of hiding from you? Do you think that you might have selected a better seat where you could perhaps see everyone?" Philip asked.

"Well, only if I sat right in the middle of one arm of the boardroom table, perhaps, but..." Cat reflected, still slightly defensively.

"But what?"

"But then I wouldn't be in the 'chair' position!" Cat stated authoritatively.

"And who says that the chair has got to sit at the head of the table, Cat? Surely it's better to sit where you can get eye contact with everyone in the team, that way you can gauge participation levels with the complete group?"

"I guess so, Phil."

"So, assuming that you spot their lack of participation at the next meeting, how would deal with Aurelie and Mario next time?" Phil asked.

"I don't know Phil, what suggestions can you offer me?"

"Well, a lack of verbal participation in a group environment is not *always* a negative sign, Cat. Some people are naturally reflective and need time to process what you are saying. But you, as their leader, need to know that they are with you, and are not going to be a negative influence once the meeting is over."

"Maybe I should just call them out in the group for being quiet and ask them what they are thinking?"

"Well, that is one option, Cat. Sometimes people are simply waiting to be invited into the conversation and if their invitation never comes, they may just remain silent. Sometimes they are unparticipative in meetings because they don't like speaking in groups though."

"So, I could ask how they feel about the things we agreed today, at their next one on one?"

"I think that might work best. That said, it's probably worth bearing in mind something that I was trained on recently. It is how we like to receive and process information."

"I'm not sure I follow you, Phil. What do you mean?"

"When two people communicate, there are two completely different thought processes happening: one from the 'communicator', the other from the 'receiver'. When you communicate, you design in your mind the message, compiling the words you want to use, the tone of voice you are going to employ and what you are going to physically do, to help communicate your message, I mean with your hands, facial gestures and so on."

"I guess so," said Cat, "but some of that is subconscious."

"Absolutely right. However, the subconscious in this circumstance, reflects the conscious thought, when the message is delivered. You will gesticulate, show enthusiasm even use the rhythm in your voice to ensure you get your message across, all of which you have designed to help the 'receiver' comprehend your message the way you want them to."

"I see that," declared Cat. "But the receiver doesn't always *get* the message!"

"That's true and that highlights the disconnection between the '*intended* message' and the '*receipt* of the message'. What's happening is that the 'receiver' has to 'decode' your message in order to make some sense of it. They have to almost put your words into a language that *they* understand. It's much like when someone is speaking in a foreign language. First you listen to identify the words that they speak; then you translate those words into a language *you* understand."

"I see, but we are all speaking the same language here, so there really shouldn't be an issue like that," Cat stated defiantly.

"True, but even when speaking the *same* language, they may even get stuck over some of the words that you use because it means something slightly different to them. It is only when the message is correctly 'decoded', that the 'receiver' has effectively understood the message."

Philip could see that Cat was deep in thought over what he had just said. He surmised that she was, in fact, decoding his words at that very moment.

"Hmm, that makes some sense, Phil. I know that on occasions I have asked my partner what I have just said to him and yet he is *unable* to repeat it word for word!" Cat eventually stated.

"Ha ha, so how do you know that the message has been decoded correctly?" Philip asked in order to help Cat think through her approach.

"Well, I would ask them questions about what I have just said, and see if they can repeat it."

"That could work, but may sound a little like an interrogation, if you're not careful," Philip joked with a smile spreading across his face. "How else?"

"If there was a way of ensuring that I could get the message in a format that the 'receiver' understood *first* time, that would certainly help."

"You've got it!" declared Philip with the enthusiasm of a salesman closing in on the sale. "So, here's something that might help you with that. There was some research conducted in California by Albert Mehrabian to understand how much of a message is received through each of the three communication elements: *verbal, vocal* and *visual*. *Verbal* refers to the words that we select, *Vocal* is the way in which we deliver those words in respect to tone, pitch, timbre of voice; *Visual* is what we do with our faces, bodies or cause the 'receiver' to *see* when we speak. Have a guess how much of the overall message, that is of the 100% piece of pie, was remembered by each of these three components?"

Philip encouraged Cat to write down her percentages for each. When she had finished, he continued.

"So, the research found the following results. What did you have for the first one, *Vocal*?"

"I reckoned it was about 40%."

"Most people put a high figure on that one, but actually *Vocal* was a lowly 7% of recall. In other words, we find it really difficult to remember the words that people use because of this decoding process our minds use."

"Oh yes, makes sense if you put it like that, Phil."

"What about the next one what score did you put against the *Verbal* element?"

"That one I had down as 30%."

"You're quite close actually, Cat. *Verbal* was found to account for 38% of the overall message. We can recall what people were saying because of the tone of voice that they use or the way that they spoke. And, finally, your score for *Visual*?"

"30% again."

"It might surprise you that most of the message is remembered from the *Visual* aspect of communication. In this research, about 55% of the message. In other words, more than *half* of the overall conversation is recalled because of what people *see*, not what they *hear*!"

"I suppose that makes a lot of sense because I get very distracted by what people wear, and sometimes lose sight of what they are saying as a result!" stated Cat with a chuckle.

"Ahh, you are not alone Cat, most of us have a bias towards what we *see*. If you remember your Bible stories, it was the same when Christ appeared to his apostles after his resurrection and Thomas stated that unless he was able to *see* him, and *touch* his wounds, he wouldn't believe. We are pretty much the same; if we *see* someone with a shifty face or a false grin, it completely distorts the message that we *hear*, and we always seem to believe what we see rather than what we hear!"

"Certainly true for me."

"That brings me on to another point. If we want people to remember what is being said, and we want them to *learn* from it, we need to acknowledge that there are basically three ways to achieve this. We have effectively spoken about two of these ways: *Visual and Audible*. People with a **Visual** bias form the bulk of the population and is the reason why TV is such a force of communication. **Audibles** are those that prefer to close their eyes to focus on what they hear. They find that they can receive greater clarity of message when the visual is negated and they can concentrate on the actual words being used, and also the way in which the words are delivered."

"Sounds like people that use the telephone well?" asked Cat.

"Yes, absolutely. They would be distracted if it was a video call though!"

"So what is the third way to receive information?" Cat asked Philip, lost in a world of thought at what she was hearing.

"The third medium that some will prefer to learn through, is touch. **Kinaesthetics** find that they need to handle something, feel it in their heart or experience it. This is so that they can make sense of it. Some artists talk about what the music or painting makes them *feel*. This is a kinaesthetic response."

"OK, so my message will be received and digested in an *Auditory*, *Visual* or a *Kinaesthetic* way. Or presumably a combination of all three? but how do I know what each of my team members prefer?" asked Cat, earnestly.

"Well, a bit of a giveaway is often in *their* use of language, Cat. You know, if you are a *Visual* you may say: 'I see' a lot, whereas an *Auditory* might use the term 'I hear what you are saying.' *Kinaesthetics*, on the other hand, might use the term: 'I feel' frequently. But that aside, you can always cater for all three forms by ensuring that there is something visual in your message, even if you are only asking them to *imagine* something. If you could give the team an item to touch or hold, the *kinaesthetic* members of your team would be happy, or even ask them how they 'feel' every once in a while. Equally, why not blend in something for the *auditory* sensors, like asking how the message 'sounds'?" Philip suggested.

"Yes, good point. Sounds easy enough," Cat declared. Then after a few more seconds of thought she added: "I guess that you can always adapt your whole communication style, if you identify a bias to one of these preferences? I mean, I am thinking of Mario who is a very emotional individual that seems to *feel* everything. So maybe I should ask him how he 'feels' about the changes, but I would never use that question for Emre, who seems to have no emotions whatsoever!"

"Totally right Cat. This is a tactic that I understand is used by the best trainers, but I see no reason why it's not relevant to every relationship and friendship, business or personal. I use it when designing training sessions to ensure that I do something to appeal to each set of receivers, and it seems to go down well. It's all about using *all* the communication tools available to us, to ensure our message hits home in just the right way."

CHAPTER 17

EVALUATION

"HR tell me that, because you've been in the role for three months now, I have to do a review of your progress, or rather, your 'performance'. That's the reason I called this meeting, Philip," Gareth stated in his usual brash manner. "Tell me what you feel you have achieved over this quarter?"

"I believe I have achieved quite a lot, Gareth," Philip stated as confidently as he knew how. "I spent a little time trying to figure out what it was that we needed to change, and then how 'training' might help that corporate shift we were looking for. I then designed training that was appropriate to the needs of each business group and finally I delivered it to each of them. If I had to do it all again, I'd have trained up the managers first, so that they could support the roll-out of the learning with their teams, once the individuals got back to their workplace. Instead, I spent time retrospectively with the managers and coached them through the implementation of our solution strategy. It all seems to have gone well, at least that is the message I am getting back from the business."

"I see," contemplated Gareth before adding: "and how do you *know* if your training has had any impact whatsoever?"

"I guess I'm expecting it to be reflected in the corporate results for this quarter. How are they looking?" Philip was eager to know, especially after he received such a hard time when the last results came out.

"The results have yet to be released," Gareth stated in his usual matter-of-fact way. "I know we have spoken of this before, but how are you measuring the success, or failure, of the training though, Philip? What metrics have *you* put in place to establish if there is any impact of your sessions?"

"I....er...," faltered Philip, feeling uncomfortable at the direction that the conversation was turning. Gareth always seemed to bring up something that side-swiped him off his feet.

"You need to bring me data, Philip, because without data I am unable to present a case for your success in this role," Gareth cut in. "Figures, anecdotal evidence, stats; without which, what you do is just a load of hot air to make people *feel* good," he stated, the last couple of words were spoken in a heavily sarcastic manner that seemed to offer a true indication of his feelings towards training.

Philip realised that he had left himself exposed through his failure to close the loop and show tangible impact from his training. Clearly, he thought, I need to work out how to produce something meaningful, that the board can accept as proof that my training is helping the business move forwards. But how?

That evening María called. "How was your appraisal?" she asked in her soft, tender voice.

"Not as good as I thought, to be honest," Philip replied without any attempt to mask his disappointment.

"Tell me why?"

"Gareth stated that I had neglected to show, through figures, graphs or whatever, that my training was having any effect on the business. He stated that he needed proof in order to maintain me in my role. I feel under a lot of pressure once again María, and it's getting me down. I mean, it seems like a huge amount of work to do for Gareth, which I would have had the time to do a month or so ago. But the fact is that now I am getting requests for help from managers across the business almost every single day. I really don't know when I will have the time to do this data-crunching!"

"I'm coming over, Phil. I can help you with this. It's not as desperate a situation as you might think," her voice was calming, with an accent that seemed to sooth and appease Philip who had been working himself up into a bit of panic.

When María arrived at Philip's house, he noticed she was wearing her 'chill out' clothing (leggings and a sweatshirt, her long black hair tied back in a ponytail). Philip realised that he had never seen her in a casual outfit before; each time they had met, she was dressed either in business clothing for work, or cocktail dresses for nights out. He noted that he liked her every bit as much like this, as he did when she made an effort.

"Open up a bottle of red then, and then we can get to the bottom of this issue," she enthusiastically chirped in a mock bossy manner, making Philip smile with a warmth of appreciation. "Do you remember a few months ago that I mentioned that there were, in fact, *five* disengaging influences causing people to fail at the role of training management?"

"Yes, of course!" declared Philip. "How could I ever forget our first meetings?"

"So, what are they?"

Philip trawled through his memory bank. It was amazing how many theories and concepts he had learnt over the last three months, he thought.

"The first one was around a *lack of research*, then *poor training design, bad delivery* was next, and then *not following up*," he eventually stated, triumphantly.

"Bueno. Well done Phil. You must have had a great mentor to learn that so well!"

"The best," said Philip as he gently pulled María's long pony tail.

"The trouble is, that's only four! Where is the fifth, Padawan?" María enquired, effecting a synthetic Spanish accent with a slight teasing tone.

"Er....I....er, I can't recall the fifth, sorry," Philip reflected, sheepishly. His brain was working overtime trying to remember what it was. He began to feel very guilty that he had not, in fact, learnt as much as he thought.

"Don't worry cariño," María was sympathetic as she consoled him, "I haven't told you the fifth and final one yet!" She giggled that her teasing had the effect she wanted.

At that, Philip flung himself at her in a mock fight, but rather than reigning blows, kisses were showered.

Eventually, when they had settled down again, María stated: "I think you have already found the last one out for yourself, actually. The last reason why trainers fail is because of a lack of *Evaluation*. Evaluating the training is an essential part of what we do for all the reasons that Gareth appears to have listed this afternoon. If we don't evaluate the impact of what we do, we are considered to be a drain on company resources, an expense. And when hard times hit the company, it is the roles which drain resources that are seen as expendable. That's why I have been made redundant twice in my career already. I suppose I have learnt the hard way that we need to constantly prove our value to the corporate accountants, and the board I suppose, if we are to survive in the good times *and* bad."

María drew on a piece of paper:

The pyramid, from top to bottom, reads:
- No Evaluation
- Failure to Follow Up
- Inappropriate Delivery
- Ineffective Design of Training
- Lack of Research

"I hear you, but the question is *how* can we evaluate training?" asked Philip.

"Yep, that is the $64 million question that seems to have baffled training managers for years. Over the last number of decades, the 'end of course questionnaire' seems to have been the vehicle of choice for most organisations. This is the form that the trainer shoves in front of you just as you are desperately packing up your things, wanting to get home!"

"Oh yeah, I never used to fill them in with any serious comments."

"And you aren't alone, that's exactly the problem with them. The information they provide is often weak because they are hurriedly completed, without much time or thought. Besides which, if you *know* the trainer is going to read what you have written, you may not always choose to be as open and honest as you should. So, the figures and comments can become distorted or somewhat unreliable."

"So why not do an anonymous questionnaire online after the event?" Philip suggested.

"We have tried that too, but came across the issue that few people, if any, actually take the time to complete the questionnaire once they have left the training room.

In fact, the completion rate dropped from 100%-if completed in the training room, to about 30%-if left until after the event. I guess people just don't have the time or the inclination when their day to day tasks are screaming at them to be completed."

"Seems like these questionnaires are a complete waste of time and effort then? I have a pile of these things sitting in a drawer on my desk; sounds like they should be shredded?"

"No, I don't think so," María was quick to state. "It is a valuable guide to assess the *immediate* reaction to the training event, but it is in no means an 'evaluation' of the training. Perhaps a better term for this might be a 'validation' of the learning, as it seems to act as a way of stating how *valid* the training was perceived to be for their role. At least on first inspection anyway. It's only once they are back in the workplace that they can really assess how valuable the training actually is to them, isn't it?"

"Yes, I guess so," Philip was thinking the matter through.

"This," María continued. "Is the first of four 'levels' of evaluation that was originally identified by Donald Kirkpatrick in 1959. I believe he published it in his book '*Evaluating Training Programs*' in 1994 by Berrett-Koehler Publishers, I have a copy if you want to read it? In his book he assessed four aspects of the training that might be evaluated, as follows:

1. "**Reaction** of the participant to the training, what they thought about the content, delivery, environment etc.

2. "**Learning** that they believe they gained from the training in terms of knowledge or capability.

3. "**Behaviour** in terms of what capability or improvements were seen as a result of the application of the learning, and finally,

4. "**Results** being the effects on the business or working environment as a consequence of the learning, as shown through the participants' performance."

"Well, that certainly sounds far more scientific than just an end of course questionnaire!" exclaimed Philip enthusiastically. "Which one is the best one to use then?"

"It's best not to look at them in isolation like that, Padawan, but rather to think of them as four component parts of the whole. In other words, the *reaction* is easy data to gather, but isn't going to give you much more data than a 'feeling on the day'. Level two, *learning,* is then more difficult to gather, and level three, *behaviour,* is even more tricky to prove. By the time you get to level four, *results,* which is obviously the hardest to collate of the lot, you have really valuable data for any business. It's like gold dust, Phil, because it is the one that organisations value the most."

"OK, so how do I go about gathering all these evaluations? You said that it might not be as difficult as I thought?"

"True. You remember the first reason why trainers disengage with the company?"

"You mean because of the *lack of research*?"

"Precisely. What research did you do at Woodroot to assess whether training was needed, and what it might do for the organisation?" María enquired.

"Well, I spoke with the senior leaders and asked them what they viewed as a good result of the changes in corporate direction. They gave me some figures based upon the increase in sales revenue, service delivery response rates and time spent with customers fixing issues," Philip recalled immediately. He had been living these issues for the past few months now and could probably recite them in his sleep.

"Do you still have those figures?" she asked.

"Of course."

"Good, because these will for the basis of your level *four* evaluation. These are the *results* that your training was designed to accelerate the company towards. You'll probably be able to gather the information on the progress towards these goals by looking at your reports, or the management system. You might like to depict the progress in terms of achievement as a percentage against the target, rather than as a bare figure?" María suggested, taking a sip of her wine.

"Yes, yes, I can do that," Philip replied eagerly. He had that feeling that one gets when the pieces of the jigsaw start to produce the whole picture. "What's more, I think we are well on target to achieve these results that the leaders wanted. In fact, we may even be ahead of the curve!"

"If that is the case, Phil, then you can shout about that because it will be down to the way you structured and executed the learning."

"Hey now, hold on. I'm not so sure I can go around making claims like *that*!"

"Why not?"

"Because the people that are out there with the customers, closing the deals, providing the solutions and backing up with efficient support are the ones who *actually* make those figures happen," Philip remarked categorically. He had always prided himself on a sense of fairness, giving credit where it was due.

"I totally agree, but look at it this way. Had you *not* have ensured that they were trained and capable to do all of those jobs, would the company have hit the targets that it has?"

"Well, I suppose not."

"That is why I can genuinely state that, without your effective training, these results would not have been achieved."

"I see what you mean," Philip had to concede the point. "But it was also down to the fact that the managers and teams actually implemented the learning."

"Modest you are, Padawan," Maria said in her best Yoda impression. "Seriously though Phil, what you say is true, but don't forget you also helped them by coaching and supporting *management* capability too."

"I guess you're right."

"So this is where you look to the level three-*behaviour*, and see what you can record as progress against changes in the 'behaviour' of those you've trained," Maria continued. "You told me you've been following up with the managers and assisting them with the implementation of the learning in their teams? What have you actually achieved in that respect?" she asked.

"I've spent a lot of time observing the leaders interactions with their teams, and then interviewing the managers afterwards. This is when I have tried to coach them in new methods to get the best out of their team members, and develop their teams' skills and engagement levels. In almost all of the cases, they have seen some great results."

"Oh? What results have you seen?"

"It depends on the team, but I've heard of better team unity, improved engagement between manager and individual, or even between the individual and the company. I've had managers telling me that the performance of their 'low performing' employees has turned around, and that they are pleased with how the group have responded to the new ideas."

"That's all gold, cariño. We need to capture all of what they have said and seen because this is all great level *three* data. It will outline the extent to which the participants to your training have applied the learning and changed their behaviour."

"Cool," replied Philip reservedly, "But how do I capture it? Most of what I've just told you is anecdotal from conversations by the coffee machine or in passing their desks!"

"In that case, we could perhaps look at running an assessment, in addition to the notes that you'll have taken from the observations? I suggest that the assessments need to be ongoing though, and over a period of time, to avoid them becoming a 'snapshot' on any given day."

"What's the problem with a snapshot approach though?" he wondered out loud.

"Simply because you might catch people on a particularly good day, or a bad one. Either way the mood on the day may distort your results. If we collect the data over a period of time, it gives a more valid and valuable reference. We will be able to highlight their change in performance and take into account anything that may be happening in the organisation or industry."

"That's a good point. I doubt I would have thought to associate this data with things that are happening outside of Woodroot Hosting."

"It makes sense and it also shows you to be thinking more commercially than you might otherwise have been."

María took a final sip of her drink and drained her glass.

"You'll need to have a think about how this assessment should be designed, but a good rule is to make it as *objective* as possible. I know that might sound obvious, but I say that because most assessments fall into the trap of being too *subjective*. Perhaps look at relevant performance scenarios using specific key performance indicators or criteria as a guide? I have a couple that we use that I can send over to you tomorrow to look at, but you'll need to design your own really because this is a very personal thing to your company."

"Thanks darling, you are lovely," Philip said tenderly, with adoration in his eyes. Once again, María had come to his rescue and had found answers to his worries that, had she not have been in his life, he would have been unable to discover. He wondered how he would have coped in this role, had it not have been for her friendship, care and attention.

"Self-assessments can be a really useful tool to use for this purpose too," she continued, seemingly oblivious to Phil's thoughts of gratitude. "They are quick and easy to set up online and can be assessed relatively simply too."

"Great idea, I will have a word with HR tomorrow and see what system they use for that sort of thing."

As if she was on a roll and wanting to ensure that all the aspects were covered, María continued with her thought process.

"Level two might be a bit trickier. We really could have used a snapshot *before* the training as a benchmark. In this level, we need to understand what impact the learning has had on the *individual*, in terms of their increased knowledge or capability. I don't suppose you had any gauge of their understanding before the training took place?"

"I didn't for most of the groups, but certain teams I did, for example the finance teams and those dealing with compliance issues. They all had to sit tests six months ago on their knowledge of certain internal and external processes and policies. In fact, I believe that they are all due to sit them again because they have to renew their licences every half year."

"Well, if that's the case, then that would be a great way to show that their knowledge has improved as a result of the training," María stated excitedly. It seemed to Philip that she too became excited as more of the jigsaw puzzle pieces were slotting into place. "In fact, you may be able to use some of your sales and service delivery observations as a guide for the future too. These will highlight how the individual has improved when you next see them. A word of warning though for these assessments at this level, they need to be closely related to the original aims and objectives of the training, if they are to prove the impact of your sessions."

"That seems logical. Gareth seemed to give me the impression that there might be a load of skepticism over the impact of my training unless I can prove it."

After taking another swig, but from Philip's glass this time, María finally looked at the last of the evaluation levels, or rather the *first level*.

"You mentioned you have a load of course 'validation' forms in a drawer of your desk. Have you done anything with them yet?"

"No, I read them of course and may have changed some of the content around as a result of their comments, but that's about it."

"OK, well this is data that we can use too. Have you structured the questionnaire so that the individuals score things out of 5 or 10?" she asked.

"Yes, most of the questions ask them to rate their experience out of 5, but then there are some free text questions too."

"Good, we can use the scores to assess overall satisfaction rates and track trends. Maybe we can break them down to specific business units, even teams? This data will highlight if there are any issues within a particular group, or business area, that need some further support. It can also be cross-referenced against the team, or business unit, performance results to see if there is any correlation there too."

As she was talking, Philip noticed her utter enthusiasm for this topic. Her eagerness to solve his puzzle was infectious, she was excited to see all the pieces coming together, and clearly visualised the resultant picture. She was truly a marvel, he thought, and here she was sitting on *his* sofa, sipping Rioja from *his* glass. He had found happiness at last.

"María," he said gravely and with the sort of hesitation that comes when one is struggling to find the right words. "You are *so* kind and *so* lovely to make this much time for me. I've been lost in this role an extraordinary number of times, and on each occasion, you have thrown me a lifeline. Had it not have been for you, I'd have made mistakes aplenty, I would probably have found myself fired by now in fact...or had a nervous breakdown. But you have always been there for me. Why have you been so kind to me?"

Clearly moved by his words, María put the glass down on the coffee table and turned to him, as they sat side-by-side on the sofa. Placing a hand in his, she spoke softly to him, looking deeply into his blue eyes as she did so.

"Phil, at the start I was doing a favour to Mo and Ashley, because they asked me to look after you. But when we talked about learning and development matters, I suppose I saw something in you that showed massive potential. I loved your enthusiasm and energy to learn, it was so refreshing and I was glad to spend time in your company just to feed off your energy. But..." she hesitated, clearly debating in her mind whether to continue or withdraw from the conversation.

"But what?" Philip enquired urgently.

"...But I eventually realised that what I felt for you was more than that. When you didn't contact me for that period..."

"Yeah, I'm so sorry about that, I was..." she touched his lips with her finger in a motion to silence him and allow her to continue what was clearly a difficult conversation for her to have.

"When we didn't speak for that period it felt to me like an eternity. I was miserable to the point that colleagues at work commented on it. It felt as though a massive void in my life had opened up and I was falling into it. Phil, I realised then that what we had was more than just friendship. You are indeed my best friend, you are the only person whose company I relish. I find that I cannot wait to see you, I adore speaking with you whenever we meet and, when we are not together, well, I just find myself thinking of things I would love to talk with you about. Sometimes I catch myself thinking of experiences I want to have with you, places I'd love to take you."

Philip noticed her eyes seemed to be gathering droplets of water at the base of each of them, welling up in the corners. These brown eyes had never looked so beautiful, he felt.

"María..," he started, before she cut over him.

"No, Phil, let me finish or I will never manage to get this out. You see, ever since my parents split up and my father left home, I have never seen relationships as anything more than close friendship. I read those fairy tales of love where princesses are carried away by their knights in shining armour and live 'happily ever after', but I *never* believed that there was such a thing as true love. I hoped I was wrong, but have never found any proof that such a depth of emotion ever existed."

A small teardrop fell from the corner of her left eye and gradually cascaded down her cheek as she spoke, seemingly unaware of it's escape.

"Phil, mí cariño, *you* are my knight and *you* have shown me that the fairy tale really does exist. What I am trying to say, in a very awkward way is.....well....that I think I love you."

Philip was dumbstruck. He had never heard such words expressed to him, and so eloquently too. The emotion with which María had spoken was greater than anything he had ever witnessed. At that moment, he realised that the girl in front of him was the girl he had been waiting for all his life, the one that he connected with on more levels than he could have ever hoped. She had brought something special to his life, something that he realised he never wanted to let go of for as long as he lived. Without thinking, he instinctively leant forwards and kissed away her rogue tear from her cheek and whispered: "María, I love you too, with all my heart. I never want us to be apart either. I want us to be together because you make me a better person, a professional trainer, you fulfill me."

The couple spent the next few minutes looking into each others eyes for some time, neither saying a word. Words were not necessary at this time. Then, sensing an air of relief that the emotions were finally open for all to see, Philip broke the silence and said in a lighthearted manner: "Now that we have got that out of the way, will you *please* stop calling me Padawan?!"

CHAPTER 18

ENGAGING INFLUENCES

"What a whirlwind of a year," Philip reflected as he sat on the top table at the Annual Learning & Development Awards dinner. The trophy for *'Best Training Programme'* stood proudly on the table in front of him. María held his hand and looked deeply into his eyes, filled with adoration and loving emotions.

"You deserve this for all the hard work and devotion you have put into it. I could not be more proud of you than I am right now, even if I tried," she said as she wiped a tear of joy from her eye.

Philip surveyed the scene which befell him, in something of disbelief after only a year since he agreed to take the role in Gareth's office. Across the table from him, Nathan was enthusiastically debating something with Eddie that their wives seemed to find extremely amusing. Beside him, Philip heard his mother and father chattering away about how lovely the food and the venue were for such an occasion. Gareth had sent his apologies for not attending, but in a way Philip was quite relieved as this meant that he was able to offer his invitations to Mo and Ashley, looking resplendent in their tuxedos and both eagerly awaiting the band striking up so that they might cut a few shapes on the dance floor.

He felt fulfilled, as though everything in his life at last made sense. Around him he had everyone that had been influential and helped him in his training career, and that felt right to him too. He turned to María and looked deeply into her brown eyes.

"Thanks darling. I meant what I said up there on the podium tonight, though. This award is down to you and your advice, your guidance and your love. You are amazing. My amazingly beautiful baby."

María smiled a wide smile, her brown eyes were pools of love reflecting his own for her.

"I'm sure you would have managed just fine without my help," she smiled.

"Categorically *not,*" Philip exclaimed. "You remember the five *'disengaging influences'* that were at the hub of our relationship last year? Well, I'm certain that I would have done every single one of them, left to my own devices. Without you to tell me what to do and how to do it, I know I would have completely disengaged the Learning and Development department from the rest of the business. But you prevented that, darling. You were always there with a practical answer to help me."

He kissed her deeply, with adoration and love.

"But there is one thing that you got wrong, you know?"

"Oh?" María looked bemused, she had no inclining that Philip had found fault with the pyramid or had changed his view on it.

"Yes," he stated emphatically as he took her hand and, using a pen, traced the outline of it onto the back of the order of service, her fingers and thumb left as an outline. Then he wrote across the thumb '*Lack of research*' and then, across each of the four fingers the remaining 'disengaging influences'.

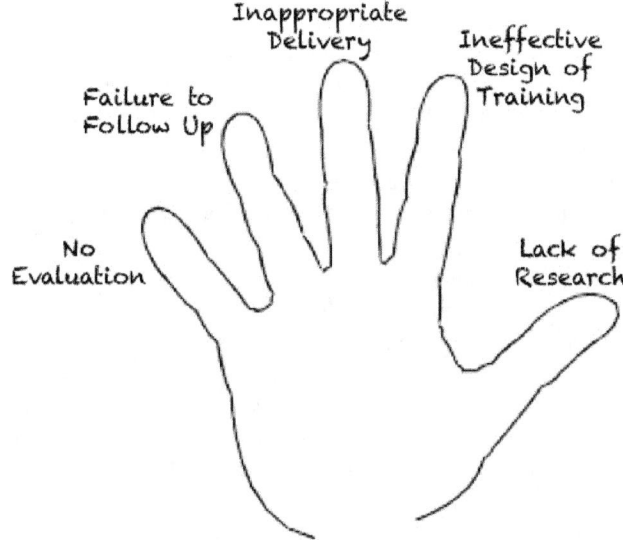

"You see darling, it's not a pyramid at all. It is a *handprint*, remember?" he smiled at her. "When we first met, you said that in training, we are leaving our imprint on the people that we train, do you recall? Well that's exactly what we do. We leave a handprint in fact. It's the result of making sure we engage with the business and the employees in each of the five 'influences'."

He touched each of her finger tips as he spoke.

"If we don't do the research up front, if we fail to understand what the business or teams need, if we never work out how we are going to align learning to the corporate or team strategy, we will forever be 'under the thumb' of the accountants, feeling as though we should be grateful for our existence because we are seen as a drain on resources. The rest of the fingers will be useless if we don't sort this out first. The thumb can exert more pressure than any of the fingers, in the same way that the business needs are stronger and more dominant than any other factor in learning. In fact," Philip moved his own thumb to press against each of his four fingers of the hand in turn. "The thumb touches each of the other 'influences'. So you see, the needs of the business, whether at a corporate or team level, have *got* to flow through the other five remaining parts of the model. None more so that this one."

He reached over the María's little finger and began to caress it with his own fingers.

"The expressed business needs that training is to address in the *research* phase, have got to directly correlate with the *evaluation* we conduct. You told me that, do you remember? This evaluation, needs to prove that we did what we *said* we were going to do. It needs to be wrapped up in data, in observations, assessments and it has to prove that we have made progress or, at least, explain why we haven't!"

He moved to her index finger, kissed it and continued to touch it with his own fingers.

"The design of the training is essential to point us in the right direction, just as this finger is deployed. We use our index finger to point things out. If we get the design wrong, we will fail to to implement anything *effective* for the business, and therefore fail to achieve the results we targeted. If that happens, we are going to be pinched between the thumb-*business research*, and this finger-*design of the training*."

María's eyes met his, she looked like she was in a daze, a dream of love, filled with admiration and adoration for the man beside her. Philip moved his hand to her next finger.

"This middle finger is the longest, the most prominent and stands prouder than the rest. *Delivery* is the part of the training that everyone sees, it is what everyone judges the whole learning experience against. Does the delivery help people to remember and learn, or is it easily forgotten? The ABCD structure is invaluable with this, it gave me a great chance to create something useful and the delivery competency framework that you and Nathan worked with me on, gave me the skills I needed at the right levels to make my delivery effective to everyone. Get this one wrong, though, and there is nowhere to hide."

Taking her next finger, brushing it against his lips, Philip stated,

"This finger cannot be neglected if we want some *long-term impact*. If we fail to *follow-up* on the learning with those that have taken the time to be trained, we won't have any long-lasting effect. I discovered that it doesn't always have to be *me* that does this, but I do have a role to play in supporting learning in the workplace. Managers coaching their teams is what makes this a valuable thing. Working together as a unit: me, the manager and their team members, helped us all to grow together, trust each other and find that we all share the same goals. Employee commitment and engagement are therefore unified; the manager and the employee create this kind of 'bond' between them because they all want the same thing. I can help by coaching the manager or even policing that it's done in the organisation, if I have to, but I prefer this part to be a partnership between the manager and the individual."

The band began to tune their instruments in the background as Philip held her left hand in his, looking deeply into her eyes. He sensed her eyes were welling up again in an emotional tidal wave.

"That is just so beautiful, Phil. You have made everything fit together like...like..."

"Like a *hand* in a glove?" he smirked.

"Yes!" she exhaled in a partly humorous and partly emotional sign, a tear flowing down her cheek out of sight from her man beside her.

"You know, darling, this finger here," he wrapped his lips around her *follow up* finger. "Is arguably the most important one of them all?"

"Oh, why is that?" she asked.

"Because this one is the one that creates something that is real, something that is strong, a bond freely entered into by two people. This finger speaks of confluence, of unity and of a deep commitment. It is *this* finger that will ultimately show whether we have left an imprint on the lives of others...and that is why I want you to wear this on yours, mí bella cariño."

Prising her eyes from his, she felt the coldness of something sliding down her finger and looked to see the engagement ring he was positioning on it. The diamond sparkled against the dancing light of the candle on the table. Tears trickled from her eyes now as she raised them to fix upon his.

"María, you were my light when darkness surrounded me, you came to me and showed me the right path when I was lost. You have been so patient, tender and kind to me as my mentor. *And* you have become my best friend, my true love. I've found someone in you that I admire, that I trust and whom I will love for always. Will you marry me and leave *your* imprint on my life forever?"

Without hesitation, María responded.

"Sí, mí amor, YES!" the tears were flowing freely now, but nobody seemed to care. "I can think of no one that I would rather spend my life with than you. You are full of surprises, Phil," she said, utterly ecstatic.

This had not only been the proudest night of her life, watching the man she had fallen in love with receive a prestigious award, but, now, it was also the happiest. As Philip started wiping away her tears that cascaded down her olive coloured cheeks, María stated with a wry smile: "I can certainly declare, that you have mastered the art of the *engaging* influences now, my handsome Jedi knight!"

COPYRIGHT

About the Author

Jonathan R. Smith is an internationally respected Learning & Development authority, organisational development consultant and talent management expert that has dedicated his life to identifying and developing the potential in people. Jonathan has built many L&D functions across a diversity of industries, using the winning formula explained in this book, *The Disengaging Influences*.

Jonathan has designed global competency frameworks and leadership programmes, high-potential identification and development processes and has toured the world delivering his *Training for Trainers* workshops, based upon the sound foundations of this book.